W9-AVC-826

CREATING INDEPENDENT STUDENT LEARNERS

A PRACTICAL GUIDE TO ASSESSMENT FOR LEARNING

Pauline Clarke, Thompson Owens, Ruth Sutton

PORTAGE & MAIN PRESS

Portage and Main Press acknowledges the financial support of the Government of Canada through the Book Publishing Industry Development Program (BPIDP) for our publishing activities.

Cover and text design: Relish Design Studio LTD.
Cover photo: Thomas Fricke
Printed and bound in Canada by Friesens

Library and Archives Canada Cataloguing in Publication

Clarke, Pauline, 1947-
    Creating independent student learners, grade: 4-6 : a practical guide to assessment for learning / Pauline Clarke, Thompson Owens, Ruth Sutton, .

Includes bibliographical references.
ISBN 1-55379-087-1

    1. School children--Rating of. I. Owens, Thompson, 1947-
II. Sutton, Ruth, 1948- III. Title.

LB3060.22.C553 2006   372.126   C2006-904219-5

ISBN-10: 1-55379-087-1
ISBN-13: 978-1-55379-087-7

PORTAGE & MAIN PRESS

100 – 318 McDermot Ave.
Winnipeg, MB Canada R3A 0A2

Email: books@portageandmainpress.com
Tel: 204-987-3500
Toll-free: 1-800-667-9673
Toll-free fax: 1-866-734-8477

Printed on 30% PCW paper.

To all the teachers of the
Winnipeg School Division
Inner City who are not
named in this book, but
who worked diligently as
we all tried to find the
best ways to help our
students succeed.

Acknowledgments

The authors wish to thank the Winnipeg School Division for permission to publish this material and, in particular, Mr. Jack Smyth, Chief Superintendent, Winnipeg School Division (1982–2002), who provided encouragement and support for the work described herein.

CONTENTS

INTRODUCTION

This book is about practical ways to help students become independent learners through *assessment for learning*. The ideas presented here come from an initiative to bring research on assessment into the classroom. During the years 2000 to 2003, 80 teachers from the Inner City District of Winnipeg School Division were given the opportunity to develop their skills in assessing their students. These teachers understood that assessment was an important part of their programs and were willing to explore their own practices and seek ways to improve. We named the project on assessment for learning *Feedback for Learning*.

This book is a showcase of the participating teachers who taught in grades 4–6 classrooms, and of their experiences with reworking their assessment practices. Along with an abundance of information about how to create independent student learners, there are many comments and examples of their observations working with students. The eight steps in the scaffolding outlined in chapter 1 and expanded on in the remaining three chapters will give teachers a guide to how to rework their assessment practice and how to think about transforming their students into independent learners. Each chapter includes rubrics, working charts, and essays, themed according to our experiences with Feedback for Learning.

In addition to the practical information on creating independent learners, we believe it is important to share some of the thoughts and challenges we encountered, in part, to allow you to see that change in any teacher's practice is gradual; it takes more time than most of us would like, but it is worth the effort. We have included essays, our reflections, to help teachers feel more comfortable and confident as they embark on the process of change.

This book can be used independently by teachers, or as the basis of a study group with small groups of colleagues. Teachers may use the whole book as a program or they may read short sections to find effective ideas that will improve student performance. The book is organized around eight steps, structured into a scaffolding format. Each step is explained and there are examples of applications from participating teachers. We have also included ideas that helped teachers as they worked through the scaffolding to try to create independent student learners. We have divided the content into the steps in the scaffolding to help build the language, experiences, and thinking skills that students need in order to be reflective learners. The students become learners as they learn to identify their strengths, weaknesses, and strategies they can use to help themselves.

This is also a book about change. We believe that asking teachers to reflect on their practice and to implement new techniques in assessment are not trivial tasks. Classrooms are very complex places and teachers must be treated as adult learners. As you read through the book, you will see that teachers were encouraged to control the pace of their work, to discuss their ideas, to deepen their understanding, and to trust their intuitions.

The path for participating teachers was not always easy but their skill, perseverance, dedication, and good humour have resulted in a deeper understanding of how to help students become independent learners and of how to improve their students' performance.

1

KEY IDEAS

Feedback is not merely useful.... It is an essential part of any completed learning.

— Grant Wiggins, 1998

Guiding Question

What is the impact on your students of your present assessment program?

Key Ideas of Chapter One

- assessment for learning helps students use information about their own learning

- the goal of assessment for learning is to help students become independent learners

- the scaffolding is a frame of essential teacher behaviours for assessment for learning

- teachers must see themselves as learners in the change process

Introduction: Why Read This Book?

The main intent of this book is to show teachers how to help their grades 4–6 students become independent learners. We want to show teachers the very specific procedures that will help students see how they learn best. Students will also learn how to focus on areas they find difficult. Finally, instead of being faced with disappointment and feeling stuck in their work, students will learn how to use multiple strategies and acquire a more flexible attitude when confronted with problems.

Students in the grades 4–6 age group are often a wonderful combination of emerging independence and excited amazement at their learning discoveries. Students at this level are a joy to teach because they keep their natural curiosity bubbling at the surface and love to ask questions. They have matured beyond their primary experience and can think more abstractly, and they have opinions to share. We will show how teachers can capitalize on these natural strengths of students to involve them in their own learning.

The disparities in student ability at this stage are beginning to widen. Teachers will find that the ideas suggested here will have the most impact on those students who always seem to perform at the lower end of performance scales. At the same time, students at all levels will benefit from the path to independence.

Many grades 4–6 students are at the transition point between elementary and secondary school. Most students must move to an entirely new location separated from the community of their elementary school that has supported them for many years. This is a major concern for teachers as they strive to prepare students for their new learning challenges. One of our main goals of assessment for learning is to create a way for students to take what they learn and use it throughout their school careers.

We believe students will be most successful in this transition if they have acquired confidence in their ability to learn. The ideas presented here will provide a basis for teachers to show students how to become independent learners. To be a continued success in school, students cannot be passive recipients of knowledge but must become active participants in their learning. Beyond the encouraging words and good intentions of the teachers, students must have the skills and confidence to deal with problems by themselves.

Finally, we want to help teachers feel successful in their own learning. Too often, teachers forget to take into account their own learning needs when teaching. It is easy to feel successful when everything is going well but it is more difficult when, because of the complexity of classroom environments, things do not go as planned. Teachers often react by working harder to rectify the situation, but find it difficult to find the most appropriate solution.

Successful teaching is not about piling more work on top of already busy schedules, but how to find the core of what is really important. We have tried to arrange the material so that teachers will be more efficient in their teaching. We have included reminders about how teachers can respect their own learning needs.

What We Mean by *Assessment*

We divided assessment into two separate categories that are different in their approach and resulting success of students. Assessment that is the administration of tests and the collecting of marks is called *assessment of learning*. In this type of assessment, the feedback is almost entirely used by the teacher and has little to do with communicating with the student. The flow of the information about performance moves from the student to the teacher (see figure 1.1). The purpose of assessment of learning is to give the teacher enough information to calculate final grades for report cards.

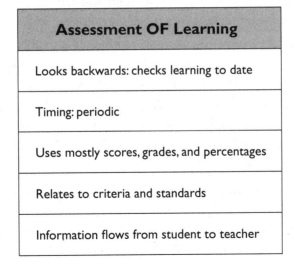

Figure 1.1 Assessment of learning.

In this book, we explore assessment as *assessment for learning*. In assessment for learning, the teacher uses the feedback and information gathered from student performance to adapt the teaching program to better meet the students' needs. The teacher helps develop the students' ability to learn. Assessment for learning helps create classrooms where both the teacher and students are able to use feedback to adjust their own performance. The teacher uses feedback to adjust their teaching and the student uses feedback to adjust their learning. An important part of assessment for learning includes those teacher behaviours that help students learn the skills and behaviours that will enable them to correct their work. For instance, students need to learn to complete their work according to the requirements set out by the teacher. Many students begin working with only a very general notion of what is expected and only stop working when they become tired or distracted. They have little direction and no targets to meet. Students need to learn to expect, as a matter of routine, that there will be more than one requirement and that, in order to be successful, they must try to meet all of them. Teachers need to learn how to help students adopt this learning behaviour.

Students do not always arrive in class with the ability to assess themselves, and so assessment for learning includes teachers' efforts to train students how to collect feedback from their work and make improvements. Teachers move away from doing everything for passive students to doing things that encourage, train, and empower those students to be independent of the teachers. In so doing, students are brought into the learning process.

This understanding of assessment includes many teaching procedures that previously might not be thought of as having much to do with assessment, such as making the assignment very clear, giving students time to think, helping students identify key factors to succeed, and giving students opportunities to correct their work. This may be seen simply as good teaching, but in terms of assessment for learning, this also serves to help students acquire the power to become learners.

When we use just the term *assessment* in this text, we mean to imply the notion of *assessment for learning*, and in particular we concentrate on the teacher practices that help students learn how to learn, such as the ability to self-correct any task. In assessment for learning, the flow of information about performance, the feedback, is used not only by the teacher but also by the student (see figure 1.2).

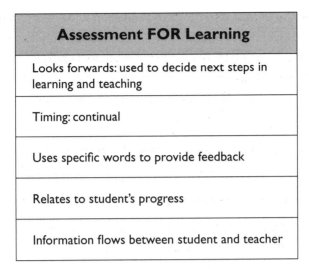

Assessment FOR Learning
Looks forwards: used to decide next steps in learning and teaching
Timing: continual
Uses specific words to provide feedback
Relates to student's progress
Information flows between student and teacher

Figure 1.2 Assessment for learning.

What Are the Student Outcomes?

As a result of adapting the assessment for learning techniques that focus on the learner, teachers will find that student performance will improve and the students will see themselves as learners.

More students will be successful in achieving the curricular outcomes as the teacher learns how to target their lessons and help the students identify problem areas of their own work. Following are some grades 4–6 teacher testimonials describing their students' progress and success in adapting the scaffolding (see figure 1.3).

> Children became responsible for their learning. Improvement/growth in writing became evident. Students who often produced work that was "good enough" (their words) began to take ownership for their writing.
>
> *– Kathleen Weir, grade 4*

> The feedback was very positive for all learners because they were involved in the process. Work habits improved. There was more effort and students remained on task.
>
> *– H. Sinclair, grades 5–6*

In addition to being successful learners, students will come to understand how they learned. Students learn how to refine their thinking about what they can do successfully and those areas to which they will need to pay special attention. Students will be able to talk about themselves as learners and develop repertoires of preferred strategies that help them when they encounter problems in their work. The assessment techniques not only result in more successful students, but also give students the tools and reflective ability to learn independently of the teacher. The students become lifelong learners.

We define a learner as someone who possesses three characteristics or skills:

1. the ability to recognize what they know or what they can do
2. the ability to identify what they are unsure of or have difficulty with
3. the ability to identify the next steps he/she needs to take, or the strategies he/she has to help with their problems

The Scaffolding Described

At the heart of assessment for learning are the teacher behaviours and procedures that encourage students to succeed in learning. All students can become learners if the teacher believes they can be successful and takes certain actions. But what are those actions?

The procedures outlined in the scaffolding help teachers transform from assessment of learning to assessment for learning (see figure 1.3).

As you read through the steps of the scaffolding, you will probably recognize many of the steps and perhaps already use some in your teaching. The purpose of outlining the steps is to help guide your thinking and choices of activities so that your programs become more efficient in helping more students become successful learners.

Assessment practices, as described in the scaffolding, fall into three main categories:

- making the target clear to the student
- practising the language and skills of knowing how to learn
- deepening student understanding of how they learn through student reflection

Figure 1.3 Scaffolding for developing student learners.

Classrooms that promote student learning are populated with students who are aware of what they are supposed to do. Student learners are created in classrooms that provide multiple opportunities for students to practise reviewing their work to look for ways to improve. Students are taught to see "being stuck" as a learning challenge they can solve in a variety of ways. In learning classrooms, students are given time to reflect on how they learn.

Helping students understand what they must do in a task is a daily challenge for all teachers. Some tasks require only a brief explanation; others require examples or demonstrations. While observing classrooms, we noticed that teachers spend a great deal of time explaining clearly to the students what must be done and making sure they have heard the directions.

In assessment for learning, *Setting the Target* has three critical procedures (steps 1–3).

    Step 1 Understand the learning task and the learning intent.

    Step 2 Share task/intent with the students in accordance with the students' learning profile. Discuss, "What will it look like when we finish?"

As part of this step, students are asked to help create a list of criteria needed for success in the lesson.

Step 3 Design and carry out enabling tasks that lead students toward the learning goals.

Let's go back and think about the teacher carefully explaining a lesson to the students. At first glance, not much changes for the teacher if the assessment for learning steps are followed. The teacher explains and the students listen. The critical change is in how the teacher thinks about what information the students will need in order to be successful – intent, criteria for success. By focusing on the task and developing the intent and criteria, students are more focused on what they need to do to be successful.

The second category of teacher behaviours, *Practice*, develops the students' skills as learners. Students need to practise assessing their own performance to decide what they have done correctly and identify those areas to which they need to pay attention. With repetition, students learn how to look carefully at the models, compare their work with the models, and decide what will improve their work. Furthermore, students need to have many experiences that will help them build a repertoire of actions and strategies.

Steps 4–7 of the scaffolding identify four teacher behaviours that help students practise being learners.

Step 4 Provide a first attempt for the students to show what they know.

Step 5 Invite comparison.

Step 6 Have students identify the next step(s).

As the teacher and students follow these steps over time and in many situations, students acquire the skills of reflecting on their work. As the students are reflecting on their work, they are also hearing the language associated with these experiences and have opportunities to practise using the words and phrases they need to express their learning.

In this stage, teachers will have opportunities to watch students carefully. This may sound far-fetched, but, by following the assessment for learning scaffolding, there will be times when teachers find they are just standing around while the students work. For example:

This morning I did a lesson on linear measurement. I used my chart paper ... explained the task.... wrote it down.... explained the purpose (intent) ... wrote it down ... showed them what was expected ... wrote it down and I sent them off.

I was sitting *alone* in my chair on the carpet. Everyone was on task and interacting and using math language. Everyone was engaged and successful! I continued to sit and took it all in.

— Teresa Campanelli, grades 4, 5, 6

After the shock wears off, these rare 'alone times' can be used by teachers to decide which students have understood the lesson and to make judgments about the learning needs of their class.

The final stage of assessment for learning is *Reflection* and has only one step:

Step 8 Encourage students to look back and reflect on themselves as learners.

It is not enough to give students opportunities to improve and to ask them to record how they improved individual pieces of work. Students need to think back on all their individual experiences to see the patterns in their learning. Often teachers jump to this step too quickly, asking students to reflect on their past work without giving them enough time to practise thinking about their work during the term. The opposite happens just as frequently. Teachers work diligently with students during the term to help them rethink their work, but then forget or run out of time to allow students to think deeply over a range of learning experiences. Students need to practise and then be given time to solidify their understanding about themselves as learners.

The quality of questions that teachers ask students will improve student reflection. Questions should be designed to help them think critically about their learning. For example, ask students:

- What are your strengths?

- What specifically seems to give you trouble?

- In what ways do you help yourself?

Teachers can also help students deepen their reflection by paying attention to the timing of their questions. Students should be given time to reflect well before the assignment is due and then asked to reflect again some time after the assignment is finished.

Where Should Teachers Begin?

It is critical that teachers be allowed to choose where they wish to begin. Each teacher will know best what they already understand about assessment and the amount of change they are willing to make. Teachers may first read over the scaffolding to find some aspect of assessment they find appealing and wish to use as the basis for their decision making.

The scaffolding makes choosing a starting point easier because it provides a framework to organize many assessment ideas and gives teachers some sense of the bigger picture of assessment in the classroom. The eight steps suggest how individual ideas about assessment practice may be related to each other and how each builds upon the other towards helping students become independent learners.

The scaffolding organizes the many ideas about assessment in the same general way a lesson is usually organized:

- the lesson is given
- the students work through the task
- there is a summary event at the end of the lesson

The scaffolding parallels these stages in three different sections: the set-up, practice, and reflection. Each stage identifies key teacher behaviours in assessment that help students become independent learners. A teacher who is planning a lesson and wondering, "What can I do to help my students be independent learners?" can refer to the scaffolding at each lesson-planning stage to help them decide which ideas to incorporate.

The scaffolding is a helpful way for teachers to begin thinking about their assessment practices. We want teachers to be able to look at a broad range of assessment ideas and select an area to work on that is most meaningful to them. The scaffolding is specific enough to be helpful but does not restrict teachers to any particular assessment strategies.

In the early stages of adapting the scaffolding, it is most helpful for teachers to analyze their existing assessment programs. Even though the scaffolding has numbered steps 1–8, teachers do not necessarily need to progress through the steps in a sequential manner. Teachers can use the scaffolding to find a way into the assessment process and pinpoint areas on which they want to work.

Each step of the scaffolding becomes a manageable target for working on assessment. As teachers experience success, they can use the scaffolding to decide what their next steps will be. The scaffolding is relatively short but contains many important ideas.

Finally, teachers can use the three-level rubric (see appendix 4) based on the scaffolding to evaluate their programs at the end of the year. In all these ways, the scaffold is a tool for teachers to help progress in their thinking about assessment.

How Quickly Should Teachers Proceed?

The short answer is that teachers should not expect to go quickly in this process. Teachers should take the long view regarding changes to their assessment procedures. There is no need for teachers to feel they must rush to complete all the ideas in the scaffolding before they see an impact on their students. The students will show immediate improvement even if the teacher tries only one or two of the ideas presented here.

Ultimately, teachers should try to use all the scaffolding steps frequently during the school year. The more teachers incorporate the scaffolding, the more independent students will become as they develop more awareness of how they learn best. This is the goal, but teachers must be realistic in the context of the demands of their school environments. Schools are very busy places. Even though assessment for learning is extremely important for the success of students, there are many other demands during the school year: attendance, reporting, special assemblies, new programs, discipline issues, health concerns, and so on. All these things also require attention and may take teachers' time and energy away from fully implementing the scaffolding procedures. Teachers need to be patient and persistent while accepting the constraints of their schools. Keep the goal in sight: full implementation of the scaffolding to create independent student learners.

By trying one or two ideas and then reflecting on the impact, teachers will be treating themselves as learners. The point of improving assessment programs is not to add one or two procedures but to rethink current practice in terms of what is known about the best teaching practices. Teachers may use the scaffolding as a basis to reflect on their assessment practices and to deepen their understanding of how students learn. Change in teaching practice is slow, complicated, and multi-layered. The reward of going slowly is that teachers can deepen their understanding of assessment so they can see adaptations and applications that go far beyond the examples we present here.

In this book, we present examples of what teachers have done to incorporate assessment for learning in their grades 4–6 classrooms and reminders of what teachers need to do in order to be adult learners. For example, adult learners need choice, time to work with colleagues, support, and an acknowledgement that change may occur much more slowly than anyone would like. Teachers will also need opportunities for discussion with trusted colleagues. Professional discussions with trusted colleagues deepen teachers' comprehension of their work. Teachers need regular support from sympathetic administrators and consultants who listen carefully, explore ideas, can act as critical friends, and ask probing questions. Finally, adult learners need time – time for the cycle of work to occur, time to pause, and time to reflect so that deeper understanding can develop.

We recommend teachers strive for change over the longer term. We hope that teachers allow themselves the privilege of going slowly, think critically about the work presented here, modify the ideas on the basis of their judgment, and look for broader applications.

No matter where teachers choose to begin or at what rate they proceed, the intent of their work should be a confirmation of the best in their teaching. We end this chapter with a statement from a grade 5/6 teacher that captures the impact of the scaffolding on her experiences in assessment.

> For me, in a word, the scaffolding was reaffirming. The scaffolding reaffirmed that the instructional practices I had been using were on the right track. It reinforced that a very systematic, deliberate and patient approach to instruction is needed in working with these students and I incorporated even more of this into my program. It provided the visible signs of success that these students desperately need to feel a sense of accomplishment.

> For the students, they have become more informed learners and have a greater understanding of what and why they were learning. They have become more empowered because when they say they are "finished" they can self check/self assess and begin to explain what they have learned and how it will help them. The concrete evidence of improvement and/or success was motivating and empowering for students. The greatest impact for students is the increased motivation that results with visible signs of success (I can). They could begin to talk about their work.

Most students were able to:

- assist in setting task criteria
- articulate what the goal and intent of an activity was
- use the criteria to self-assess their work (this took much guided practice)
- complete the task with greater success – more confidence (less task avoidance)
- articulate what they could do to improve their work
- demonstrate pride in their work – big smile, willing to share with classroom teacher

Students who were less motivated to learn were able to:

- focus more readily on what they could do
- be redirected more easily and positively when an activity was challenging or understanding broke down
- demonstrate a greater willingness to talk about their learning in a positive way

– Sharon Baetz, grade 5/6

Self-Review: Setting a Baseline

We invite teachers to spend some time reviewing their current thinking about assessment before moving ahead and adopting new processes. By reviewing their present practices, teachers can gauge their progress as they work on improving their assessment programs. It is difficult to celebrate success when you cannot remember where you started, or see what has changed.

> The teachers we worked with in Feedback for Learning were given three years to develop their programs. This was in no way too much time. Many teachers reported that they felt they really did not fully understand the work until the second year. Even though we understood that we needed to be persistent, no one was happy with the pace of the change.
>
> Our experience has shown that changes to teaching practice come only when the teachers take the time to pause and to reflect on their learning.

When we began working with teachers, we asked a set of questions for self-assessment (see figure 1.4). Surprisingly, no matter what grade level or subject taught, from nursery school to grade 9, all the teachers responded similarly to the questions. They all believed that assessment was essential to student learning, they all regularly shared their learning goals, and all of them involved their students in self-assessment. Furthermore, most of the teachers believed that their students were capable of improving, and provided daily feedback for review by both the teacher and the students. However, our own observations of their classroom practice did not match what teachers reported in their self-assessment questionnaires. How can this discrepancy be explained?

Original Questions for Self-Assessment

1. How important is assessment to students' learning?
2. How often do you share your learning goals with your students?
3. How often are your students involved in self-assessment?
4. What percentage of your students is capable of improving?
5. How often are you able to provide feedback?
6. How often do you have a chance to reflect on students' assessment data?
7. How often do your students have a chance to reflect on assessment data?

Figure 1.4 Original questions for teacher self-assessment.

We have come to understand that teachers tend to respond to pre-assessment questions in terms of their own beliefs and what they want to happen in their classrooms, not necessarily what actually happens. Although their beliefs are central to a good assessment program, it is more helpful to teachers if they can identify the concrete ways their teaching time is devoted to student assessment that increases learning.

Self-assessment questions should also elicit what teachers actually do in assessment. Their responses mark the beginning of a change process that deepens a teacher's understanding about assessment, enriches their practice, and aligns their day-to-day practice more closely with their beliefs.

We suggest choosing one of the best lessons or units that works well for you and use it as the focus for the self-assessment questions. Then, use these questions as specifically as you can to record what you actually do in the lesson in terms of assessment – questions you ask, activities you organize, or handouts you give to students.

After thinking about the questions and writing a few answers, add two dates beside each question (see figure 1.5). The first date will remind teachers of their initial thinking about the questions and the second date is a promise to revisit the self-assessment questions to think about next steps. Teachers should be generous with setting the second date so that they can proceed slowly but deliberately to improve their practice before they reassess.

1. How do I make the learning objectives clear to my students?

_____

_____ Date: _____ Date: _____

2. What activities do I use to help students improve their work?

_____

_____ Date: _____ Date: _____

3. What questions do I ask to help students think more deeply about their work?

_____

_____ Date: _____ Date: _____

4. In what ways do I help students see themselves as learners?

_____

_____ Date: _____ Date: _____

Figure 1.5 Questions to ask before starting the process of change.

Our Reflection

The ideas in this series arose from a three-year program to help teachers develop their assessment techniques so that student performance improved and students came to see themselves as learners. Another strong theme that developed was that teachers needed to be treated like learners themselves if we wanted the ideas to be sustained.

At the end of each chapter, you will find an essay on one of the four main ideas that guided us as we developed a program that respected the needs of adult choices. We assume that the principal audience of this book will be classroom teachers and so each essay is written with them in mind. We hope teachers will learn from our experience to enhance their own journeys as they deepen their understanding of the art of teaching. However, all educators can read these essays as they try to design programs that not only help students but meet the learning needs of the teachers in their schools.

Time: An Essay

We advise that before you begin too much work on your assessment practices, you should consider how much time might be involved. The length of time required to accomplish change depends upon the depth you want to achieve. If you simply want to try out a few ideas, your time commitment will be very brief. If, however, you want to develop a deep understanding of the ideas presented here and apply them in many aspects of your teaching, you must allow yourself much more time. The length of time involved in the process of change is often underestimated. Without a realistic sense of how much time and effort are required, you might become frustrated at your rate of change. We want to emphasize that this process is lengthy, yet is exceedingly rewarding in the end.

We understand that we are rarely allowed the luxury of time. It is very reasonable that the people who implement new programs want to see results as quickly as possible. Generally, when there is a new initiative in a school division, the amount of time allowed for implementation is shorter than anyone would like, and certainly shorter than needed to make the best of the change. The cost of training teachers is very high. Efficient introduction of ideas and quick implementation are very important criteria when programs are designed to introduce new ideas to teachers.

As a teacher, you have a responsibility to yourself as well as your students. You have many programs already in place and many obligations to fulfill in your classroom. One basic question you should consider at the beginning of this process is, "What are your present commitments?" You cannot simply add something new to your plate and suppose that you are going to carry on trouble-free and succeed. The burden inevitably becomes too much so that every time you add something to your workload, something suffers.

You have learned that to be successful in the classroom, you have to develop procedures to be a successful manager. The procedures are habits that you have developed over the years through trial and error. Most teachers are not even aware of many of their routines because they have become habit. The habits save you from having to reinvent the wheel all the time, but they also do not change easily. It will take more time to understand how to accommodate the new ideas in your classroom situation and adapt them to your own style. Adaptation requires thinking. The more time you have to think, the easier it will be to make the changes.

It is not unreasonable to give yourself three to five years to come to a true, deep understanding of any new idea. Consider the first year as a general introduction. You spend your time getting a good feel for what is involved. You learn the vocabulary and try out a few things. Often, one problem in the first year of change is that the best ideas usually come after you have already made plans for what you wanted to accomplish and have set up routines for your classroom. Working around what is already established will make it more difficult to implement change. As a result, even though you might strongly believe in the work, you might not have a great deal to show for your first year of change.

Even though we began the work on assessment as a three-year project, and we had made this clear, all the participants felt as though something was wrong at the end of the first year because there was very little evidence of change. Teachers enjoyed the conversations and felt engaged in the work we were doing. They tried a few things in their classrooms and were pleased with their work. Still, there was a feeling of disappointment. The general feeling was that there should be more to show for all the work they were doing. Always, the push is for results over understanding.

After a year of introduction, the second year always seems much easier. You will feel more confident with the ideas about the program. This year you will do it right! And this is generally what happens. In year two, many of the early questions have been answered, so implementation will seem easier.

You are learning and you can expect to encounter difficulties because there will be things you had not considered. It is all part of the process, but the errors tend to stand out more than what you did right. Even the best teacher will have ideas that didn't work, students they didn't reach, and ideas they didn't get to because they ran out of time, money, energy, or all three. It would be a mistake to assume you are going to master these ideas in two years.

In year three, your learning is at yet another stage. The lustre has worn off and the new idea is no longer fresh. You are beginning to realize that the new techniques are not the complete answer to teaching. Experience has turned activities into tools for helping students. In year three, you can refine your ideas and the worksheets to make them better fit the needs of your classes. You question whether it is really worth the effort to pursue this particular educational approach. You are better able to see the shortcomings of your approach and see the modifications you need to make. In the third year, you can look for ways to adapt the basic ideas to areas of your program. You are making the ideas your own as your understanding deepens.

Year three comes with its own special set of problems. Teachers tend to forget what they didn't know when they began so long ago and to downplay the advances they have made. Even though you have made significant gains, your achievements may not be near your original goals.

This is the nature of change.

So give yourself time. It is time to go deeply into one idea, such as assessment practices that will help students become independent learners. As you go deeply into one idea, you will see threads of connections to other ideas. Mastery is a worthy goal and time is your friend.

2

STUDENT LEARNERS

If you don't know where you're going, any road will get you there.

– Randy Bachman, 1992

Guiding Questions

1. In which other ways could you describe a learner?

2. What would be the benefits/drawbacks of making "self-esteem" your main teaching goal?

3. What is lost if you set "improving grades" or "improving student performance" as the only goal for students?

4. How would our definition of a student learner help with school portfolios?

5. How much time should you set aside in your planning to allow for building the language of reflection in your students?

Key Ideas of Chapter Two

• the target of assessment for learning is to create independent student learners

• teachers must incorporate student reflection at the planning stage

• questions should lead students to think about how they learn

• carefully chosen questions can deepen student understanding

• ask students to answer questions during the unit and again at the end of unit

• quality thinking takes time

Introduction

We begin our journey at the end of the trip. We want teachers to embark on their exploration of their assessment practices with the final destination in mind. The final outcome must not only be that students show they have learned the skills, concepts, and ideas of the lessons, but they also must see themselves as learners. All the other steps in the scaffolding should be seen as building towards success in this final step. This chapter is about helping teachers form a clear picture of what a student learner looks like. It is a fundamental principle of learning that says, the clearer the target, the greater the success in hitting the target.

In terms of our scaffolding (see figure 1.3), this target is listed as step 8:

> **Step 8:** Encourage the students to look back and reflect on themselves as learners.

Most students in grades 4–6 are only beginning to show signs of being independent of the teacher. Students at this level can sometimes be asked to work by themselves or in groups without constant monitoring. At other times, teachers will run themselves ragged trying to help all the students who need attention.

Steps 1–7 are designed to help the students reach the goal in step 8: being independent learners. The first seven steps provide the daily procedures that develop students' ability to work on their own and deal with many of the problems themselves. The more teachers use steps 1–7 in their daily routines, the more they will find their students are able to solve their own problems. Instead of immediately calling for the teacher when they encounter a problem, students will develop strategies to help themselves. These steps will be discussed in more depth in the following chapters.

In step 8, students are asked to think about their learning in a bigger sense than being just one or two lessons and to talk in general terms about how they learn. The purpose of asking students to think and talk about their learning is to make them more deliberate learners. Helping students be more articulate and specific about their learning abilities increases their ability to deal with future problems that will occur from one unit to the next and from one year to the next. Students move beyond strictly emotional responses to finding more thoughtful approaches to solving problems in their learning. When teaching students in grades 4–6, it is not as simple as just saying to the students, "Now, go reflect on your learning!"

In this chapter we will discuss what it means to encourage students and identify what students need to know about how to look back and reflect successfully.

Definition of a Student Learner

Let's begin with defining what we mean by a *student learner*. Any student who has shown mastery of the curriculum content can be considered a learner. We take this definition one step further and suggest that a true learner is a student who both masters the curriculum content and understands how he/she has come to learn.

It is possible that a student can learn a task or skill without thinking about how it happened. We envision students with increased reflection and awareness being able to carry forward their knowledge of how they learned so that they are better prepared for the new learning challenges they will meet in subsequent grades.

Our definition identifies the key characteristics of a student learner:

1. **Possesses the ability to recognize what they know or what they can do.** Students must be able to see and recognize that they can do some things well. The first part of the definition of a learner is particularly important for students who have had little success in school. Weaker students wrongly believe they cannot do anything well and that if they were smarter, then learning would be automatic. The teacher's job is to draw the student's attention to their specific strengths and to do this as often as possible.

2. **Possesses the ability to identify what they are unsure of, or have difficulty with.** A student learner recognizes that it is normal to get stuck while working on a task. They accept that they will encounter problems and something may not have an immediate answer. They know that if they persevere, they will find a way to solve their problem and move on. Students who do not see themselves as learners tend to see problems as a whole and they either get it or they don't. They do not know how to break their problems down into smaller, more manageable, parts. Teachers can help students refine their thinking about problems by reviewing key aspects of the task/intents with students (step 1 of the scaffolding).

3. **Possesses the ability to identify the next steps or has strategies to help with difficulties.** Successful students are capable of identifying parts of their own work that need to be improved. Successful students also have a

variety of ways to help themselves when they come up against a problem. Less successful students need to be taught the skills of reviewing their work critically and need help to build repertoires of problem-solving strategies.

An example of a student learner

Jesse was a grade 4 student we interviewed to find out how he saw himself as a learner. We began by asking him what he thought he was good at doing. He responded:

> "I can write letters. It's fun. I can mail them. I want to be a writer. Sometimes I get stuck with spelling. I wasn't sure where to put the apostrophe."

We then asked Jesse to talk about what he did when he got stuck.

> "When I get stuck I ask a teacher, or use a dictionary, or look around the room (to see if the word is written on the wall somewhere), or think, or sound it out."

Our final questions prompted Jesse to think about his favourite strategy and its limitations.

> "I like sounding it out the best because you just say, *B-U-H, A-H, T-A-H* and then write it down. It's better than asking all the time. Sometimes a letter can't be heard: sure, for example. It sounds like you are saying, *S-H-U-R-E* but it's not really. The *H* is silent, it's not actually there. It's *S-U-R-E*.
>
> And sometimes you hear a letter but it's not there. Like in steal, you can't hear the *A*. It's silent. 'The first one does the talking and the second one does the walking.'"

> *– Jesse, grade 4 student*

We can see from his responses that Jesse is clearly a learner as we have defined it. Jesse knows his strengths and areas he has difficulty with, and has multiple strategies he can use when he gets stuck. As he spoke, he took his time to give thoughtful responses and was obviously proud of his knowledge of how to be a successful speller.

Jesse was very specific with his strategy examples. The strategies he listed were obviously an active part of his learning in the classroom. As Jesse told us about the strategy of looking around the room to find a word he needed to spell, his eyes were scanning the room for an example. After he spotted a poster titled, "How to Write a Legend," he said, "Like, if you wanted to spell *legend* you could find it on a poster and spell, *l-e-g-e-n-d.*" Not only was Jesse a successful speller, he was deliberate in his learning and demonstrated ownership of his success. He clearly understood how to draw upon an appropriate strategy from his repertoire.

Implementing Step 8: Points to Consider

In the first two years of working with teachers, we discovered that most were not asking their students to reflect on themselves as learners. We had encouraged teachers to choose where they wanted to begin on the scaffolding, and most had concentrated on developing their practice using the first seven steps, which had shown improved success in student learning.

Using the first seven steps, teachers had developed their students' reflective skills and language, although they did not ask their students to explicitly talk or write about themselves as learners. Often, the teachers could not understand why they hadn't followed through to step 8, even though they knew the students' ability to talk about their learning was important.

There is a practical reason why teachers might find it difficult to ask students to reflect on themselves as learners. Reflection often comes near the end of a unit, and endings are almost always frantic in any classroom. The end of teaching periods always seems to come up much more quickly than teachers expect and there is a rush just to get everything done on time. We suggest ways to help teachers get through the hubbub at the end of a unit and include reflection as a large part of creating student learners.

Begin at the planning stage

If teachers are wondering how to fit student reflection into their program, they might consider beginning by including reflection as part of a unit they are planning. A unit of work, spread over several weeks, gives teachers more time. Instead of trying to fit student reflection into one part of one period of one day, the teacher has more opportunities to introduce reflection and to plan for multiple opportunities for students to reflect.

> The unit planning model that we most often used was based upon the Understanding by Design (UBD) model of unit planning (Wiggins and McTighe, 2005). We found it worked best for helping teachers plan for student understanding of themselves as learners.

It may first appear to be adding more work to an already crowded schedule, but it will result in less work for the teacher as students become more successful learners. Without adding student reflection to the written unit outcomes, the tendency is to treat student reflection as an option that is often left to near the end of the unit. The end of the unit comes in a rush and suddenly there is no time to ask students to reflect on their learning. Including student reflection at the planning stage helps teachers mentally prepare themselves for the inevitable interruptions and distractions that are always a part of grades 4–6 classrooms.

In figure 2.1 we offer examples of how three teachers introduced student reflection into their units. In all three cases, they added the particular outcome, "Learners are reflective." The teachers found this statement enough to prompt students to begin thinking about reflection. As the unit progressed, the teachers spent time exploring what students knew about reflection and their experiences with it.

When teachers are choosing the outcome statement, we suggest starting small for the first few units in which students are asked to reflect on their learning. As their understanding of their learning increases, the reflection goal can become more sophisticated.

We also suggest scheduling specific reflection times for students while planning the unit. When teachers are just starting to ask students to reflect on their learning, the schedule should be whatever seems most manageable. Reflection could occur once a week, once every two weeks, or, perhaps, a third of the way into the unit. Whatever the teacher chooses, the schedule will probably change somewhat, but having a schedule increases the chances that student reflection will occur regularly.

To make reflection an integral part of the unit, we also like to post the following questions somewhere visible to the teacher: "Are students learning?" and "Are students thinking and talking about their learning?" Posting these questions helps teachers sort out the hundreds of details that fill their day. If the questions are in a place where they will catch the teacher's eye, they will help teachers make decisions about what deserves their attention most.

Unit: Collaborating with Nature (grades 3, 4, 5, art and language arts)

Understandings:

☐ Expressive artworks and writing can represent understanding of nature and the elements of art

☐ Learners are reflective

– Valerie Block, Lidi Kuiper, Julie Perrin, Kathy Weir, Barb Thompson

Unit: Mystery Plants (grade 5/6, science and language arts)

Understandings:

☐ Classification is based upon a rational system

☐ Close observation requires time and careful student to find details

☐ Learners are reflective

– James Gray

Unit: Graphic Explanations (grade 5/6, math)

Understandings:

☐ Graphs can help make sense of data collected

☐ Learners are reflective

– Amie Johnston

Figure 2.1 Sample unit objectives, including student reflection.

Design questions for reflection

While there are no bad questions in teaching, some questions are certainly more productive to ask than others. Good questions can expand students' exploration of themselves as learners and encourage them to investigate their learning strategies more deeply. If our target is to have students who are independent, then the questions about learning should be designed to encourage students to think about the ways they see themselves as learners. The best questions will help students find their own path.

Keep in mind the definition of an independent student learner to help clarify the target of assessment for learning. Some of the questions should direct the students to think about how they are meeting the guidelines in our definition of a student learner. Teachers should ask students a range of questions about their learning, but there should be a core of questions related to the teacher's definition of a learner.

We defined a student learner as a student who has three distinct abilities:

- the ability to recognize what they know or what they can do
- the ability to identify what they are unsure of or have difficulty with
- the ability to identify their next steps or has strategies to help them with their difficulties

Using this definition, we designed the following questions to help students sort through their experiences to find evidence that they are learners (see figure 2.2).

Reflecting as a Learner

Name:_____   Date:_____

Grade:_____   Subject/Unit:_____

Think back on the work we have done over the past little while.

What are you good at doing? _____

_____

What do you find most difficult?_____

_____

What strategies do you like to use when you are stuck or having difficulties?_____

_____

Figure 2.2 Questions to guide reflection.

We suggest teachers base the core questions on their definitions of a student learner. They may find, as many of our colleagues have, that even if they decide to use our definition of a learner and the questions in figure 2.2, the questions are not quite appropriate for their students. Figures 2.3 and 2.4 provide teacher samples of how the wording of the questions can be changed and still help the student think about the important aspects of being a learner.

DURING

Name: _____

Date: _____

Grade: _____

Task/Unit: _____

1) What is the best part of your work?

2) What is not as good as you wish?

3) What did you use to help you make things easy?

4) What strategies could you use to help you with the difficult part(s)?

5) What else could you do?

Figure 2.3 New strategy questions for an art class. *Lidi Kuiper, grades 3, 4, 5.*

1) What is going well? What is the easiest part?

It was going well when I was wrighting.
The easiest part was when I was moding. And when
we branstormed.

2) What is the most difficult part(s)?

I had a hard Time in doing (what) because it is hard
to See what a recycling bin is made from brood.
it is spraypainted.

3) What strategies are you using?

I stop and think about it or I read the instrctic
I also look around the classroom for clues.

4) Why did you choose the strategy (or strategies)?

Because it help's me when I stop and think
when I read the instructions and when I look
around the classroom for clues.

5) What other strategies might you have used?

I asked a teacher if I did not know the questio
or I skip it a went to the next one.

Figure 2.4 Questions for grade 3/4 students. *Lyn Peterson and Pat Deluca.*

The questions were worded carefully to match the ability levels of the students. In both examples, the first three questions follow the same pattern. First, they encourage students to think about their strengths. Then, they ask students to think about where they had problems. Finally, students are asked to think about how they helped themselves solve a problem. In figure 2.4, there are two questions that ask students to think about how they found help. Question 3 is more concrete and question 4 is made slightly more abstract by using the word *strategy*. (The teachers were confident that their students were comfortable using *strategy*.) In both figures, the teachers added questions as they progressed to try to help their students reflect. In the next section we will discuss other questions that teachers could use to challenge students to reflect more carefully.

Deepen student understanding

Asking students to reflect on their learning will help them begin to see themselves as successful learners. Questions help students organize and value all their experiences as learners. The first student responses represent the beginning of their journey of becoming lifelong learners. Once the process of questioning and thinking has begun, teachers will want to think about how they can help students deepen their understanding of themselves as learners.

In any grades 4–6 classroom, a review of all the reflection sheets would show a range of responses. Some students leave the questions blank; some give only very general answers such as, "I like math" or "I don't like spelling." At each grade level, one or two students will give insightful responses that show they already have a sophisticated understanding of themselves as learners. Programming to meet this diversity of abilities and understanding is always a challenge. Teachers may wish to ask themselves the following questions to help decide what modifications they should make to their programs:

1. Did the students thoroughly understand the intent of the questions?

2. How many times did students practise answering reflective questions?

3. Did the students have sufficient time to respond?

If students are omitting responses to questions or giving answers that show they do not understand the question, then teachers may reconsider how they present the intent of the questions to the class. The problem may be that teachers are verbally explaining the intent and need to consider using another modality. It may simply be a matter of writing down the intent or using a drawing or symbol instead of just telling the students verbally.

Teachers have a tendency to rush through the explanation of the intent because they want students to begin the task. This problem may be solved if teachers decide to spend more time reviewing the intent of the lesson, and to check with students to see if they understood.

Any classroom routine takes time to establish, and answering reflective questions should be viewed as part of the new routine of learning. Minimal student responses may simply be a result of needing time to adjust. Students generally need several experiences to see exactly what the teacher means by a question such as, "What are you good at doing?" Teachers can help students by scheduling more opportunities for students to reflect on their work.

If students feel rushed to answer questions about their learning, they will give very superficial answers or not answer at all. There is a rhythm to the way grades 4–6 students go about their work. When students are given a task, the classroom seems hectic and scattered. One by one, students begin to focus and then the work is started. If students are not given enough time to settle, most of the class will have trouble getting started. Demanding quality reflection of the students requires teachers to follow the learning pace of their students. Once the students show they are comfortable with reflective questions, teachers can begin to think about how they can help their students think more carefully about how they learn.

Let's review for a moment how we get students to this point. We began by first carefully defining a student learner. We then designed questions that would lead students to our defined target. Once students demonstrate to the teacher that they have a basic understanding of themselves as learners, the students are ready to move to the next stage. The students are now ready to deepen their understanding of themselves as learners (see figure 2.5).

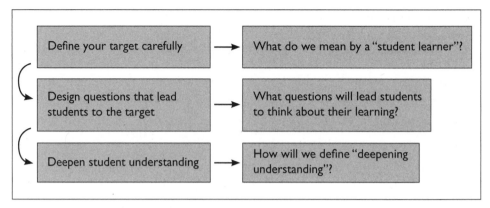

Figure 2.5 Guiding questions for developing student learners.

Teachers must answer the question, "What do we mean by deepening student understanding of themselves as learners?" We asked our students to explore several different areas of their learning process. We asked ourselves if our students were able to talk about their choices and explain their answers. Were they aware of more than one strategy? How many strategies did they know about? Had students made a connection between the strategies they like to use and their own learning styles? Had students thought carefully enough about particular strategies to be able to discuss their advantages and disadvantages? Could students use strategies in multiple situations (Fogarty and Stoehr, 1995)? In Figure 2.6, we list the main categories and some questions used to help students investigate these areas with the explanation section of this chart. Any of these questions can be followed up with a tag question such as, "Can you tell me about it?" Many students will need further prompting such as this to help them to elaborate on their one-word answers. Have students work in groups at first to help each other see how to respond to these questions. Once they see other students' responses, they will become more comfortable answering.

By asking students for *multiple possibilities* to address the task, we are asking them to build flexibility in their thinking about how to solve problems. Teachers can help students be very specific by referring to the strategy they are using while talking with students and having students record the strategy on a list on chart paper.

When teachers want ...	Sample Questions
Explanation	How do you know? What can you tell me about it? What was that like?
Multiple Possibilities	What else could you do? (repeated several times) Can you tell me another way to solve the problem? Do you remember any other strategies that might have worked? Using the class list of strategies, which ones could have worked for you?
Exploration of Learning Style Preference	Why did you choose that method? What do you like about the strategy you chose? Which strategy is your favourite? Which strategy seems easiest to you? Which strategy do you use most often?
Perspective	Do you remember any problems you had using the strategy? What might other students find difficult using this strategy? When doesn't the strategy work?
Transfer of Learning	How could you use your favourite strategy in another subject? Have you ever used _____ outside school? What can you tell me about it?

Figure 2.6 Questions for deepening student understanding.

Explaining how they learned; a good example

Students in a grade 5/6 class were asked to identify several mystery plants the teacher had brought to class. Students decided together how they would proceed with the identification process. They decided to make charts of their observations and then try to group the plants according to their similarities (e.g., flowering, non-flowering, indoors, outdoors, and so on). Students observed, sketched, and talked about the plants together. At the end of the unit, the students were asked which strategies they had used to identify the plants. Some students were able to state very specifically at least one way they found to help them identify the plants. For example,

Student A: Looked, smelled, touched the plants

Student B: We talked about it to see everyone's different point of view

Student C: Looked at pictures, books and chances to sketch and identify the plant

The student in the following example is aware that there are many options for her to complete her work. Her explanation for using the strategy is rudimentary ("it's easier"), but she shows a readiness for more in-depth comparison of other ways of collecting data when she suggests alternative strategies.

> **Student response showing multiple possibilities; a good example**
>
> In a unit on graphing, students in another grade 5/6 class were asked what strategies they had used to gather and sort their information. One student responded:
>
> > I used a table, that's about it. I used a table because it is easier to collect the data that way. I could have used a T-Chart, thinking bubbles, and a web.

Students are more effective learners when they are aware of their learning style preferences. Students need to understand that one strategy may work well for others, but might not work well for them. Focusing on style preference helps students expand their thinking from simply finding the answer to thinking about the process of learning.

Helping students see issues in perspective sharpens their thinking about their learning. Any strategy will have strengths and weaknesses of which students should be aware. Students are learning that they should always look for different perspectives and should evaluate both sides. All students will benefit from whole-class discussion of this topic to gain perspective.

Transfer of learning is probably the most important category in terms of creating student learners. Can students use their learning from one experience to reflect on another? For many reasons, teaching the transfer of learning is often omitted. Teachers can help their students by modelling this kind of thinking when they talk about different strategies. They can then question students to prompt them to think about how they can apply what they've learned to other parts of their lives or other subject areas.

Start small and go slow. Teachers should remember to be patient and gradually incorporate how they will help students deepen their understanding of themselves as learners. There are many ways teachers may choose to begin:

- select only one or two categories to begin

- post figure 2.6 on your desk as a reminder of the questions you want to ask students during the day

- begin by asking the whole class the questions and copying only the best answers

- add one or two questions from figure 2.6 to the question sheets, each time you ask students to complete their reflection

- model the thinking from one category in your lessons and tell the students what kind of thinking you are modelling

Figure 2.7 is an example of a questionnaire designed for a grade 6 class to test the depth of student understanding.

Reflection of your Learning

Name _Reva_   Grade _6_

1. What are you good at in school? _I am good at multiplying & dividing 1x2 digits or more. I am good at spelling words & reading them._

2. How do you know? _I mostly get them all right when we have tests on them I pass._

3. Do you ever get stuck? _Yes. I do get stuck when I don't know a multiplication q. and it holds up the whole q._

4. What do you do to help yourself? (Strategies) _I think about a lower multiplication question & add the rest. In L.A. I need to sound it out. Science I look back a earlier work._

5. What else could you do? _Ask a friend. Or even an adult. Sometimes I use a multiplication chart. Or calculator._

6. Which is your favourite strategy to use? Why is that? _I like to look back at present work. It helps prepare me for the next yr. And I like finding things._

7. Are there any problems with your favourite strategy? Explain _Yes. If I don't have any work to look back at then I can't do it._

8. Could you use your favourite strategy in different subject areas? Explain _Yes. I can use it math, science, LA, Health._

Figure 2.7 Reva's responses about how she learned.

Looking closely at Reva's answers, you will notice she is able to respond to all the questions. She recognizes her success in math, spelling, and reading, and gives clear explanations. She describes how she got stuck in a very specific way: "I don't know a multiplication (fact) and it holds up the whole question." She identifies several specific ways she helped herself and identifies a favourite strategy, "to look back at earlier work." Reva clearly understands the limits of the strategy and that it can be used in other subject areas as well.

From her responses, the teacher can see that she meets the definition of a learner. The next steps for the teacher include helping Reva recognize that her responses show that she is a learner, and then providing more opportunities for her to build upon and extend her present understanding of both content and the process of learning.

Time the questions

The final day of the unit is not the best time to ask students to reflect on their learning. It is just too hectic. We want to capture the students' immediate thinking but also want quality reflection. One teacher divided the final reflective questioning into two parts. The first stage of unit reflection occurred on the final day; the second stage followed the deadline and gave students a chance to reflect more on their learning.

> When you end a unit of work everything is really crazy. The kids are excited, trying to do everything. I experimented with asking them about what they learned. As they were finishing up I give them a short questionnaire to answer on coloured paper. These questions helped my students identify the problems they had during the unit while it was fresh in their minds [see figure 2.4]. I collect these papers as part of the assignment and tell the students to think about all the ways they might solve the problem. I think it kind of sets the problem in their minds so they can think about it.

> *– Lyn Peterson, multi-age class, grades 3, 4, 5*

This teacher has observed her students carefully and noted their agitation at the end of the unit. Her students' thinking is centred in the present as they rush to hand in everything. She recognizes that this is not the time to ask them to think carefully about their past experiences. She asks only a few short questions (see figure 2.8) that would help students organize their thinking about the unit experiences.

While Students Wrap up Their Work

Name: ______________________ Date: ______________________

What went well? ____

What did you find the most difficult? ______________________________

Figure 2.8 Questions to ask as the students wrap up their work.

Some time after the students have finished their unit, this teacher encourages them to think more carefully about themselves as learners.

> A few days later, when things have settled down a bit, I return the initial reflection papers to the students along with a second page of questions on different coloured paper. This time I ask the students to work in small groups and to think about all the ways they could have solved the problems listed on the first reflection sheet. They are way more relaxed and their answers show more thought.
>
> – *Lyn Peterson, multi-age class, grades 3, 4, 5*

With the students in a calmer frame of mind, and with some distance from their work, they are presented with a second set of questions. The second set is written on different coloured paper to help them organize their thinking (see figure 2.9). The students work in groups to support each other and generate multiple possibilities for solving issues they have identified after some time between the end of the assignment and reflection stage.

Some Time after the Unit

Name: ______________________ Date: ______________________

What did you find the most difficult? ______________________________

What might you try next time? (What strategies might you use?) ____________

____

Figure 2.9 Questions to ask students some time after the end of the unit.

Choice: An Essay

In our conversations with teachers, we realized that teachers wanted help finding places to begin and help getting over the emotional impact that accompanies each new request to change.

Adult learners must find ways to choose their own entry point, but some choices offered to teachers are too broad. Most in-services given to teachers contain too many ideas. In most respects, in-services are usually very positive events. You see colleagues you haven't spoken to in a long time, and the presenters are energetic, talented people with packets of good ideas. At the end of the day of in-service, you feel pumped, ready to go back into the classroom, recharged with enthusiasm with a surfeit of ideas from which to choose. The next day the packets of ideas are placed in a filing cabinet or a box, or on a shelf, never to be opened. An idea or a strategy may be wonderful in the abstract but you have to make it fit into your already busy program. To fit the new idea or strategy into your program, you need a level of understanding that is not always possible to achieve in a one-day introduction. Too many ideas do not help teachers make choices.

Our first in-services followed this pattern. We had distributed excellent resources and teachers came away from the day feeling very positive. The ideas were research-based and were presented clearly in an engaging manner, but they were too broad for teachers to absorb in one day.

The scaffolding was used to give teachers more manageable choices. The scaffolding was broad enough to give teachers a general understanding of the big picture of assessment practices after one or two opportunities to review it. It was specific enough so that teachers could recognize some elements of their own teaching. Teachers chose points of entry based upon how they could most easily adapt or modify what they were already doing.

The choices presented to teachers can be too narrow. Supposing a principal approaches a teacher and asks, "Would you like to participate in ...?" Is this a choice? Can a teacher say "No" to the principal? Many teachers feel it would be unwise to decline. Some feel they will lose their job or a transfer will be blocked, or their evaluation is this year, or they want to seem like team players. All these anxieties, largely imagined, prevent teachers from seeing the question as an opportunity.

Administrators we worked with were surprised when we shared this point of view. When we began our program, we had asked the principals to recruit only interested participants from their schools. In a few instances, the principals approached teachers directly. In good faith, they genuinely believed they were giving teachers a choice when they asked them if they would like to participate. The administrators only asked because they respected the teacher and believed the opportunity would benefit the teacher. It is an unfortunate dynamic that teachers feel they have to second-guess their administrators. The net result is that teachers feel they have little choice when asked by an administrator to participate.

Over the course of your career, you will be introduced to many new programs. However, only in the rarest of circumstances will you be asked if you want or need the program. They will just arrive. The problem is further compounded by the number of such programs that come at you like waves on a beach. All will have educational value and all will be introduced with the purpose of improving the educational experiences of your students.

As a professional, serious about your responsibility of educating young people, you might be forgiven for being resentful. On the one hand, you are told to be responsible for your classroom, and then, on the other, it seems as though you are being told you are not responsible – do it this way. In our work we tried to avoid this scenario by asking schools to volunteer to work in the program. In the first year, 4 out of 21 schools chose to participate and, in the second year, 6 more schools were ready to take part.

New programs are introduced on the basis of "rational" premises. The educational ideas are sound and, therefore, it is reasonable that teachers should want to improve their teaching in this way. Rationally, the ideas make sense. But, everything we have learned about the brain tells us there are no purely rational ideas. All ideas have an emotional component that may prompt an adverse reaction.

Even if your classroom practices are not up to the latest research findings, you value them because you have put a great deal of effort into making them work. You may feel that the new program devalues your sincere effort to do a good job. You may also feel that you are being asked to add another task to your already overburdened schedule. However you may feel about being put in this position, it is left to you to manage this emotional impact.

Reminding yourself that this is a normal reaction will help somewhat. You may also remind yourself that you are part of a large, complex system in which decisions must be made and that it is impossible to consult each teacher individually beforehand. Share your frustrations with trusted colleagues. It is not complaining; it is dealing with an honest reaction. Much of our time as support people to teachers was spent in listening sympathetically to teachers share their anxieties about their work. These feelings had to be expressed and honoured before any progress could be made.

When you feel you are ready, look for choices that are available to you. You may not be able to accept all the ideas presented at first, but undoubtedly you will be able to find something. As you look through your options, distinguish between what you must do and what you will choose to learn in some depth. As a teacher, you have developed an instinct for what will help students. Use this experience to guide your decisions about aspects in which you are genuinely interested. Search out ideas that will help your students be more successful and your job easier.

What you choose to learn may seem small at first, relative to what you are asked to do, but eventually it will have far greater impact than if you didn't make a choice. Choose from a position of strength, based upon what you already know. Choose an area in which you feel you still have room to develop. Choose something knowing you won't get it exactly right the first time but you will be willing to persist and adapt as needed. You will come to a deeper understanding of the issues involved and your teaching will become stronger.

Not only can you control what particular aspect you are going to work on in depth, you can also choose the rate at which you deepen your understanding. Your progress in any one area will be affected by your range of commitments. If your responsibilities extend over many tasks, then, of course, you must lower your expectations in any one topic. Slow it down, go carefully.

As support persons, it was our job to convince the teachers that our work wasn't just about "doing something"; we were asking teachers to "rethink" their practice. In our conversations, we would ask them to talk about what they were already doing in assessment and help them to see parallels to what was outlined in the scaffolding. These conversations clarified and strengthened the ways in which they were already helping their students become independent learners. With this approach, almost all teachers we worked with were able to choose an area they felt would benefit their programs.

Creating Independent Student Learners

You can practise this process using this book. We invite you to read over this book and choose a point of entry. What strikes a chord of familiarity? Congratulate yourself for what you are already doing to make students independent learners. Do you want to spend more time developing what you are working on now? How might you adapt a particular idea to your work? No matter where you start, as you dig deeply into any one area, you will find the one idea that will eventually lead you to all the other ideas in this book.

Choose to be a learner with your students.

3

CLEAR TARGETS

The main problem is that pupils can assess themselves only when they have a sufficiently clear picture of the targets that their learning is meant to attain.

— Black and Wiliam, 1998

Guiding Questions

1. What part of your program is the best place to start working with task, intent, and criteria?

2. Do students who can't read benefit from the intent being written out?

3. When is the best time during a lesson to introduce the task and intent?

3. What images/symbols can be associated with each criterion?

Key Ideas of Chapter Three

*   students need to know "why"

*   task and intent should be posted

*   students should help define the criteria for success

*   the Task/Intent/Criteria model increases student success

Introduction

In chapter 2 we identified the target of assessment for learning as developing student learners. In the next two chapters, we will review the first seven steps of the scaffolding, which identify the daily assessment procedures that build students' skills for reflective learning.

In this chapter, we will show the connection between the first three steps of the scaffolding and the first part of our definition of a student learner. In our definition, student learners must be able to recognize that they have the ability to learn and can back up their belief with evidence from their school experience. Steps 1–3 of the scaffolding help teachers set clear targets for students so that there is maximum opportunity for students to succeed. Good assessment begins with clear targets.

The scaffolding (see figure 1.3) breaks the task of developing targets into three steps.

Setting the Target

Step 1 Understand the learning task and the learning intent.

Step 2 Share task/intent with students in accordance with the students' learning profile. Discuss, "What will it look like when we finish?"

Step 3 Design and carry out enabling tasks that lead students towards the learning goals.

Steps 1–3

As teachers move through steps 1–3 of the scaffolding, the responsibility for learning is transferred to students. Of course, it is the teacher's responsibility to decide what students will do and what will be learned from the activity. The teacher then begins to share the responsibility for learning with the students by describing the task and what they wish students to learn. It helps to invite students to describe how they will know they have done a good job. The teacher's short lessons are focused on providing the vocabulary and skills that students need to work independently of the teacher.

For each of the three steps, there is a brief discussion, along with some good examples for teachers who have worked through the process. We also include some ideas through the process that helped teachers with implementing steps 1–3.

Step 1: Understand the learning task and the learning intent

Teachers must clearly understand the task and the intent of the lesson. The task is the activity that engages the students and the intent refers to what we want students to learn from working on the activity. Teachers are most adept at making the task clear for students. Well-ordered classrooms do not just happen; they are the result of many hours of preparation by the teacher.

Teachers know how easily grades 4–6 students are distracted, and how the omission of a small detail of planning can destroy even the best lesson. The focus becomes on organizing the school day. Defining the intent of a lesson raises the teacher's thinking beyond simply getting the job done.

Certainly, successful teachers at the grades 4–6 level have well-developed routines and transitions between the routines to help bring order to the school day. The expectations for behaviour and procedures for daily routines structure the day for students, reduce their anxiety, and help them focus on the task at hand. Teachers' thinking tends to be operational (e.g., what supplies are needed, will there be enough time, what adaptations are needed for which students). Moving 20 students in and out of activities takes a great deal of energy and thought by the teacher. However, if the classroom consists simply of well-organized routines, teachers will not be satisfied. There must be meaningful activity occurring. Rather than being engaged in mindless activities, students should be deeply engaged in learning. Only the deliberate and careful identification of what the teachers want their students to learn in the daily routines will help reach this goal.

A clearly stated intent for a lesson can dramatically lighten a teacher's workload. Teachers often try to deal with their increased workloads by piling on the objectives of a lesson and layering them into complicated structures that look good in the lesson plan but are very unrealistic, given the fact that students can only learn at their own pace.

When teachers try to cover too much in a lesson, the teacher becomes exhausted, and feels unsatisfied and unsuccessful. Not only is this unhealthy for the teacher, it is bad pedagogy for the student. The teacher can design effective lessons by continually asking, "What do I want my students to learn?"

A good general rule to remember is that the smaller the learning steps, the more chance for students to succeed. If the learning steps are too small, though, the students will not be sufficiently engaged. The teacher selects the learning intent to make the step challenging for the students but also manageable.

Clearly identifying the task and intent helps the teacher answer the question, "To which areas should I pay attention?" as the lesson progresses. The intent can be seen as being at the centre of the wheel of classroom activity and distractions. As the wheel of activity begins to accelerate, the hub remains steady. Once the class begins working, the teacher can be easily distracted by the random energy of the students, who act and talk independently of each other. With 20 students in a classroom, all pulling in different directions, it is paramount that teachers have a focus that will pull the class together. The class may be distracted from their work, but with the centre of the lesson fixed in the teacher's mind – the learning intent – it is easier for the teacher to decide what to do to get energy on task. The teacher can decide to redirect or calm the students so that they can focus on the learning. In some cases, the teacher may decide that the noise adds positive energy, that learning is occurring, and there is no need for intervention.

Teachers usually know the intent of the lessons they plan to teach. The teacher's intent, however, is not always in the forefront of their mind. When asked, teachers can explain their thinking. Usually they have several intents for each lesson. This is especially true of experienced teachers. They have taught the lesson several times, know it thoroughly, and understand its rich potential. Often, teachers attempt to meet too many intents at the same time, with the result that many things are touched on but little is being repeated and very little is being taught. The teacher ends up feeling frustrated because they tried to cover too much in too little time and they were dooming themselves to failure. Do less. Narrow the intent of the lesson to one or two points. Focus on them. Be ready for the teachable moment but concentrate on the learning that should occur.

For any task, multiple intents are possible. It is up to the teacher to decide which intent is most appropriate for that class of students. One event that may have several intents is the school-wide assembly. Teachers are often asked to have their class perform at school-wide events and must decide which students will perform and what they will be learning.

Possible intents:

- to share with the school what we have learned in our unit

- to entertain other students in the school

- to make the younger students interested in our unit of work

- to make older students amazed at how much we have learned

- to learn how to speak clearly and how to stand proudly

Any one of these intents is legitimate and valid for students as personal learning goals. Each one of the intents listed above requires a separate list of skills to be successful. Combining several intents makes the activity more complex and the chances of success go down. The teacher should choose one or, possibly, two intents that will be helpful to the students and within their capability. Trying to do too much may result only in making the teacher and the students frustrated instead of celebrating student learning.

In one grade 5 class, the students were responsible for a presentation in a school assembly. The teacher decided to use the assembly as an opportunity for students to grow as learners.

Task: To prepare a presentation for a school assembly

Learning intent: To develop and use criteria in order to enhance the assembly performance

– Linda Thomson, grade 5

The teacher helped the students focus on the learning task, despite their anxiety of performing in front of their friends. Students' thinking shifts away from showing off, or being funny, to using the criteria to monitor their own part in the production and being sure their part is as good as they can make it.

The content was made secondary; the quality of the performance was stressed. The point is that the teacher made the decision for the class, based on her perception of the needs and interest of the class.

Teachers shouldn't hesitate to use an intent that may sound general. It is true that students benefit from very specific intent statements, but if teachers wait until they get the perfect statement of the intent for the student learning, they may never use intent with a class. The general statement will still have value for teachers as a guide to their thinking during the class. After some time, teachers can make the intent more specific.

It is not unusual for teachers to modify the wording of their original intent of a lesson. In another grade 5/6 class, the students were working on a poetry unit, and the teacher shared the task and intent of the unit with the students.

Task: Write a variety of poems, using specific elements of literature (similes, metaphors, personification, etc.) that create pictures in the mind (imagery) and relate to the five senses. The poems will be shared with parents as a celebration of our learning at the end of the unit

Intent: Develop descriptive writing skills and expand your vocabulary

The unit was very successful with students and the teacher repeated the unit in the following year with another class. This time the task and intent were written:

Task:

1. To write poetry that demonstrates our ability to "think outside the box." To be creative
2. To choose words that create pictures in a reader's mind
3. To share our unique voice through poetry

Intent: To gain confidence as writers through the process of writing poetry

– James Gray, grades 5, 6

The second wording of the task is much sharper, more succinct. The intent is more focused: the students will not only learn new skills, but they will gain confidence in their writing so that they will want to write more.

Thinking about the intent of a lesson helps the teacher as well as the student. The teacher considers, "What do I really want for my students?"

In the case of this poetry unit, the time spent on task and intent was made especially worthwhile when one student wrote:

> Poetry is like my hand talking to the paper.

As much as we want students to achieve independence, the learning in the classroom begins with, and is the responsibility of, the teacher. The more clearly the teacher understands what the students must take away from the lesson, the greater the chances of students' success.

> One source of examples that elementary teachers may want to explore is Shirley Clarke's *Targeting Assessment in the Primary Classroom*. This book is filled with examples of teachers sharing the task/intent with their students. The reported results are astounding.

Teachers were most successful at finding the intent of a lesson when they were planning collaboratively with one or more colleagues. Teachers would be engaged in planning a unit they were excited about, when one of them would ask innocently, "Why are we teaching this?" The question was almost always met with silence as each one thought carefully about the "intent" of the work. The level of thinking shifted to a new level and, slowly, ideas emerged and then were refined. Someone would write down the collective answer at the top of the page and the group could move on with a deeper understanding.

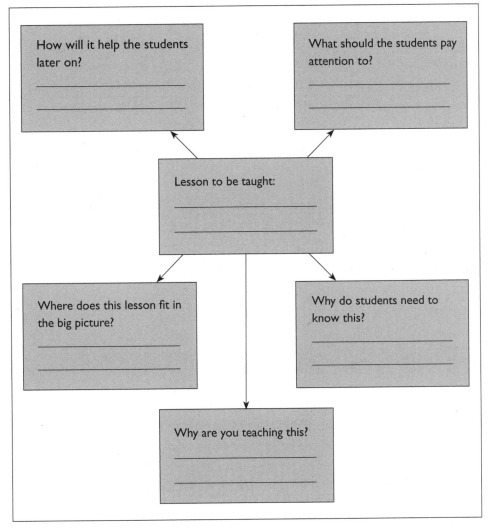

Figure 3.1 Finding the intent of a lesson.

Figure 3.1 may help you think about your lesson in terms of its intent. There is no need to fill in all the boxes; the answer to any of the questions can be your intent. If you use the form more than once, you may find one question better than the others or that different kinds of lessons need different prompts. Pass the form around to your colleagues and use the group's brain power to help you in your busy day.

Step 2: Share task/intent with students in accordance with the students' learning profiles. Discuss, "What will it look like when we finish?"

In step 1, teachers spend time thinking about what is to be learned – the intent – and how the learning will be achieved – the task. In step 2, teachers begin the transfer of the responsibility of learning to the student by introducing and clarifying the task and intent with the students. More students will have a positive learning experience when they have a clear idea of what they are supposed to accomplish.

Step 2 has two main parts:

- sharing the task/intent with students
- helping students develop a sense of ownership

In general, teachers understand the need to explain the task clearly to students, but we found that teachers had to "come to believe" the value of sharing the intent with students.

> At first, I thought that sharing the intent of the lesson was irrelevant. The first time I did it, it felt awkward. It seemed I was doing all the talking. After the first time they started to contribute suggestions as to how we would achieve my intent.
>
> – *Joan Tohme, grades 5/6*

> I am surprised by the student interest in the "why." Students don't like surprises; they need consistency and repetition. Knowing the "why" helps me in teaching.
>
> – *Kristi Brandstrom, grades 2/3*

> I previously believed that too much information about intent and outcomes might put students off but in fact it's motivated them. It has "stimulated

interest." Students are now asking for more work and suggesting new ideas. This is especially true of the more advanced students.

– Penny Davies, kindergarten

The intent is always important. In the complicated environment of classrooms, the intent of the lesson narrows the focus for students so they have a better chance to understand what is to be learned. Implementing this step takes time – not as long as teachers might think – but the results will be powerful: more students involved and more students succeeding.

How a teacher shares task and intent is important. In step 2, we use the term *students' learning profile.* We use the term to capture the variety of ways students take in information and the multiple ways students prefer to express their ideas. The complexity of receiving and giving information has been variously discussed as learning styles, learning modalities, multiple intelligences, and in many other ways. Teachers know that when they "share" with students, they may do it verbally, by writing it down, by using symbols or images, or by some combination of these. Teachers may also appeal to kinaesthetic learners by having students manipulate objects or having students move through the steps of the lesson.

One of the straightforward ways to accommodate varieties of learning profiles is to have the task and intent written out. Teachers do give clear verbal instructions to students, usually unambiguous, using language appropriate to their students, stressing important words, and often repeating key ideas. Even so, a significant number of students are visual learners and will benefit from a written task and intent.

Consider the following example from one grade 5/6 class. The students had been collecting data from various sources and the teacher wanted the students to put the data on one page so that the class could decide on the next steps. The teacher explained this to the students and wrote the following on the whiteboard:

Task: In pairs – take the data from the small pages and put it on chart paper

Intent: To experiment how we might show the data

A good job: The data is complete, clear, well-organized

– Teresa Campanelli, grade 5/6

It was important for the students to realize they were "experimenting" with organizing their data. It didn't matter if there were words crossed out or other small errors; the material only had to be readable to the other classmates. Students had to pay attention to how they were arranging the data on the chart paper.

Even though the teacher had repeated the word *experiment* in her instructions to the class, several students missed this critical part of the instruction and wanted to re-do their work when they made a mistake. Rereading the written intent helped them get on track. The written intent helped the students understand on which areas they needed to focus.

As part of step 2, teachers should invite students to think about their finished products. The teacher asks, "What will it look like when we finish?" The question invites the students to think about the assignment in their own terms. In order to answer this question, students must search in their memory for similar assignments and compare them to their present work. As the students suggest points they believe are important, they are developing their sense of ownership for the work. Listing criteria for finished work helps students reframe the assignment according to their own experiences. As students think about the final product and describe it in terms of key points, they clarify the task and think about the work with their own ideas.

Figure 3.2 offers a structure for recording the TICs in your classroom.

TIC Talk

Task _____ "Do"

Intent _____ "Think About"

Criteria _____ "Look For"

_____

_____

_____

Figure 3.2 TIC Talk: Recording the task, intent, and criteria of a lesson.

Getting started is always the biggest hurdle. Teachers may want to begin with some activity that will be repeated over several weeks.

Many teachers begin their work on assessment with this step, especially the second part, which asks the student, "What will it look like when we are finished?" As part of two grade 4 classes' writing program, the teachers discussed with the students what would make a good editor. The list (see figure 3.3) was written in student language and was used throughout the year. The list was numbered so that students knew the order of the steps to take. The "tools for revision" in step 1 were posted on a chart in the classroom. These were a list of symbols to help students identify areas that needed editing: underlining to indicate a need for capitals, circling words for check for spelling, and using symbols for new paragraphs and punctuation.

1	Used all the tools for revision.
2	Checked and corrected spelling using a dictionary. Corrected all mistakes.
3	Read over your work at least 3 times. Added more detail.

Figure 3.3 Editing criteria. *Justin Perrin, grade 4.*

The teachers found that

> The editing list worked for nearly all students. The list gives students a guideline to follow. They must think/assess what they have done. They are more conscious of the whole editing process.
>
> *– Justin Perrin, grade 4*

Another possibility to help teachers start writing out the task, intent, and criteria (TICs) is to have someone else – a teaching assistant, a student teacher, or one of the students – write them out as the teacher speaks to the class. Not only will the students benefit, but the teacher can use the written statements as feedback to ensure the instructions are accurate and complete. The teacher will see almost immediately the impact on the students.

Teachers may also use special events as opportunities to work with students on developing criteria. The list can be developed with students over some time. Teachers can begin with only one or two criteria and build up the list according to the strengths and needs of their students.

In one grade 5 class, the students were responsible for an assembly presentation. The teacher worked with the students to develop a set of criteria in order to enhance their assembly performance. As the students practised, the criteria list was changed: items were added to the list and others modified. The criteria became a useful tool to help students develop their presentation skills (figure 3.4).

Criteria for Assembly Presentation

Cooperation
- cooperate
- listen
- do our best
- pay attention
- dont shuffle papers
- be ready
- each student should do his or her part!

Speaking
- speak loudly
- speak clearly
- expression

Body language
- look at the audience
- no fidgeting
- hands at side
- be a close group
- stand still
- stand straight

Figure 3.4 Criteria for assembly presentation. *Linda Thomson, grade 5.*

As a result of the use of the criteria to hone their skills,

> The students felt prepared for the assembly. They were focused and on task during the performance. The shyer, quieter ones were able to express themselves clearly and loudly. Once the assembly was over they felt they had done a good job – they had met the criteria.
>
> *– Linda Thomson, grade 5*

The first few times teachers work with students in developing criteria will require a lot of class time. This can be discouraging for teachers, but once students get the idea, they will develop criteria much faster than before.

It is not an absolute rule that students must always be part of creating the list of criteria for daily assignments. There will be many occasions when it is very reasonable for the teacher to simply write out a few key points. Students may have completed similar assignments very recently or the work may require only a quick response from students.

There are pitfalls, however, if teachers create the list of criteria on their own. Even though teachers break the task down into what they believe are reasonable steps, it is very easy to underestimate how specific they need to be. Time and again teachers reported to us that they were "blown away" by how small the steps had to be for their students. So be warned that there is a learning process here for both student and teacher.

Step 3: Design and carry out enabling tasks that lead students toward the learning goal(s)

Our understanding of this step has changed since we first began working with teachers. We first believed that step 3 was simply about a teacher teaching "the lesson," which was distinct from creating student learners. The actions to prepare students to be learners occurred before the lesson (steps 1 and 2), and afterwards, by helping students to reflect on their work (steps 4–8). Originally, we had included step 3 so that teachers could see where the traditional teaching of the lesson fit with the work of creating independent student learners. As we watched our teachers work in the classroom and talked with them about their understanding of step 3, we refined our thinking. We now understand that the lesson is very closely tied to the task, intent, and criteria. The TICs help the teacher structure the lesson so that the lesson becomes shorter and more to the point.

Step 3 can be seen as the "how" of completing the task. In steps 1 and 2, students learn the "what" and the "why" of their work, and in step 3, students are helped with "how" they can go about their work. In step 3, the teacher practises particular skills, helps students recall certain information, or builds students' vocabulary. Students may have an opportunity to rehearse how they will go about the task.

> The term *enabling task*, originally coined by Wiggins and McTighe (1998), stresses the connection between a learning activity and the learning goals.

As the lesson proceeds, the teacher refers back to the task, intent, and criteria to show how the points of the lesson will help students be successful. Lessons are designed to enable the students to be successful at achieving the intent, the learning goals. Clarifying the task/intent/criteria sharpens teachers' thinking about their lessons. The teacher understands more clearly what to emphasize, what to repeat for the students. The teaching becomes more efficient and, consequently, much shorter. As one teacher explained, "I am more explicit and specific now."

How will a teacher know how well their lessons fit these general statements of step 3? We can't give specific guidelines, but we do know there are hints that suggest the lessons are not fully successful in realizing step 3.

Our first hint: the whole-group lesson is over seven minutes. Our general observation of grades 4–6 classrooms is that teachers spend too long with students at the beginning of the lesson and cut into the learning time of their students. Teachers tend to be over-specific and over-detailed in the lesson. Teachers' conscientiousness works against them as they try to make certain that every student knows every detail. The seven-minute limit helps the teacher remember to restrict the lesson to the essential ideas when instructing the whole group.

Of course, there are many exceptions to the seven-minute rule. Teachers may be reading to the students from chapter books. Students may become excited by a topic and their inquiry carries them long past the rather arbitrary seven-minute rule. Also, grades 4–6 students still need time to feel connected with their teacher by meeting in a group to talk about class experiences.

The point of the rule is to help teachers align their lessons with the task, intent, and criteria of the learning goals. Teachers may want to change the rule to 10 or 12 minutes. If we want students to be learners, they need the maximum amount of class time to work independently.

Here's another hint. Sometimes the teacher's lesson is a string of the following: "Pay attention," "Eyes front, please," "Are you listening?" "This is important." In this case, teachers are spending as much time trying to maintain student attention as they are teaching. Perhaps many students in the class have short attention spans, which makes it difficult for them to sit and listen in a group. Perhaps some of the students are kinaesthetic learners and need to move to learn. Whatever the reason, teachers should consider using the task/intent/criteria formula to shorten the whole-group lesson. This will allow the more independent students to start working, and then the teacher is free to provide support to other students.

This may all seem too much for teachers: shortening the lesson, writing out the task and intent, including students in deciding the criteria for success. It is too much if teachers try to change everything all at once. But, if teachers persist and slowly make changes to their instruction practice, they will see wonderful transformations in their students.

In a grade 4 class, the students were going to videotape small plays about different subjects. The students were familiar with the video camera and writing plays. The teacher wanted the students to use their skill to show, in a dramatic form, what they had learned in their studies. The first step was to have the students practise writing plays based on a school subject. After explaining the task to the students, the teacher wrote on the board:

Job (Task)	Criteria
1. Choose from a math section	Something you can demonstrate
2. Write a script	Self-edit, student edit, adult edit
(Why: To help you rehearse)	

– Rhett Turner, grade 4

After some time, the students began to line up in front of the teacher because they wanted the teacher to read what they had written. Instead, the teacher pointed to the criteria written on the board and asked, "Have you done what you need to?" That was usually enough to send the students back to their desks to go over the work themselves and find a classmate to help them edit. The teacher also noticed that after two or three students had returned to their desks, the rest of the class automatically turned to the written instructions. Students were coaching each other to look at the board to find the answers.

Having the task/intent posted in the room shifts the focus away from the teacher. The teacher then can take on the role of supportive coach. The more independent students can refer to the TIC Talk chart and leave the teacher more time to work with students requiring more personal attention.

In a grade 5/6 classroom, the students were given a series of art lessons on making realistic animal drawings with pencil and watercolours. The intent of the lessons, as described to the students, was to learn the skills and techniques of drawing realistically. As students completed several different sketches of animals, the art teacher helped them to look for various geometric shapes. She talked to them about the different kinds of lines they could use, how to create movement, and the effect of dimension in drawings. After the students had completed one drawing, the teacher's role was to help focus the students' thinking of what to do in the next drawing to improve their work. The art teacher and the classroom teacher used a series of questions to coach the students to make their own decisions.

> The students could articulate changes made in drawings from first to last. They could identify what they had to focus on in order to make a realistic picture. The weakest/least confident students were affected most!
>
> *– Sandra Buckberger, Lidi Kuiper, grade 5/6*

This shift in thinking was not an easy process. Teachers reported that "even though it didn't feel right at first," they were allowing students to make more decisions about their learning. When teachers allowed themselves to rethink what it meant to be a teacher, they experienced an emotional boost. Teachers felt they had "turned the load on the students" and this "took the pressure off."

Step 3 is the final stage of clarifying the target for students. The series of steps begins with the teacher's taking time to decide what they want the students to learn in the day's lesson. In the lesson, the teacher draws attention to parts of the target that students may not have noticed, reminding them of similar experiences or referring to strategies they can use if they have difficulties. The teacher deliberately refers to the task, intent, and criteria, which have been previously shared with the students.

The reward for teachers and students is a classroom where students are successful – learning and being independent.

Support: An Essay

The quality of our achievements in Feedback for Learning was due to the dedication of the teachers involved and the support they received. The teachers we worked with carried the main responsibility for developing and changing their own practice. Much of the work they did was on their own. They did the reading, they did the thinking, they implemented the ideas, and they found the energy to maintain their regular classroom obligations. We were able to support these teachers in several ways.

We recognize that teachers have little influence over the extent or quality of the support available to them, but a good skill is to recognize effective support and adjust your expectations accordingly.

It is possible to achieve a level of success by working alone and using the steps outlined in this book as a resource. You will see gains in student performance and your students will grow as student learners. You will have to persevere on your own to sustain your interest over the length of time it will take to explore these ideas fully.

Support from several different administrative levels can give you materials, time to think, and conversations that will stimulate your progress. From the point of view of the teachers in the Feedback for Learning project, the most obvious support came from conversations with two distinct support people. One was from outside the district and the other was already a teacher in the district. Having these two types of support people proved to be very effective.

The specialist from outside the district, Ruth Sutton, had a deep understanding of assessment and an extensive knowledge of the supporting research. Ruth was able to share this expertise directly with teachers in a manner that made teachers feel she was a colleague and a friend. Ruth made it clear at the planning stage that implementing new assessment practices was also about changing teacher behaviours and that we must treat teachers as adult learners. These ideas were carefully considered and became major components of the program.

The second support person, Thompson Owens, had worked with many of the teachers for some time and had built up a rapport and trust with them. In conversations with teachers, Thompson brought his understanding of how students learn and how educational systems work.

In the beginning, Thompson played the role of project manager: arranging schedules and helping Ruth understand the nuances of the district. Since Ruth only visited the district three times a year, Thompson maintained continuity with teachers and administrators in the interim, troubleshooting and having ongoing conversations with teachers. As time progressed, Thompson played more of the consultant role to teachers and administrators.

At least one of the support people tried to meet with the teachers about every six to eight weeks. In these conversations the support people concentrated on listening to the teachers. They used their understanding and experience to ask questions that would help teachers focus on critical issues.

The consultants avoided handing out activities or giving advice. The support teachers assumed that most teachers probably have more activities stuffed away in cupboards than they could ever use anyway. It is not the activity that is so important, it is the ability to think like the person who created the activity.

Advice had limited value. Each classroom is a unique blend of the school milieu, the particular students, and the particular teacher. Advice is an easy answer that may have worked in another context but will almost never fit a particular teacher's personality, talents, or needs.

The next important level of support for the teachers we worked with came from the school administrators, such as the principals and vice-principals. The administrators remained visible but stayed on the sidelines most of the time. They did not try to micro-manage the teachers. They showed their support through informal discussions and questions. Administrators promoted teacher discussions. They scheduled the meetings and found the funding to cover missed classes. Teachers were able to have conversations with the consultants and not be distracted by their busy classrooms. Later, discussions were arranged between staff members.

The administrators who worked with teachers in the Feedback for Learning project were patient and enthusiastic. They were anxious for results but respected the learning process for their teachers by giving them years to make progress in the new assessment practices. Finally, administrators showed support to their teachers by applying the principles of Feedback for Learning to their own practice. They treated themselves as learners and asked, "How can I apply the principles of good assessment to my work as a school leader?" This sent a powerful message to their teachers that the work on assessment was important.

Most teachers do not think of their superintendents as being a support because they seldom have the opportunity to work directly with them. In the Winnipeg school district where Feedback for Learning occurred, the superintendent, Pauline Clarke, was an important support, and she played several key roles in our project. At the start-up stage, Pauline made sure that there were clear targets, and that funding and support people were in place. As the program developed, Pauline found time to meet with the key people to listen and ask questions. The questions helped the project organizers think carefully and develop a more balanced program. Pauline was careful to follow the learning process, allowing schools to choose to participate. She was also crucial in ensuring that the program continued over a number of years and developed a sustainability plan to allow the changes to become permanent.

You may not have all these people to help support radical changes to assessment practice in your school or school system, but you will probably be able to find some support. For example:

- Are your friends willing to work with you on assessment?

- Are there colleagues, other than personal friends, who might be interested in working with you on this topic? They do not necessarily have to be in your school.

- Are there consultants in your district who might be willing to coach you? They do not necessarily have to be experts in assessment, but they do have to know how to listen and how to use questions to help clarify your thinking.

- Is your administrator open to requests for time to meet with colleagues? Can they help you find the funding?

- How might your superintendent react to a letter outlining what you plan to do, your intent, and your self-evaluation scheme?

Review your support options and rate your situation. If some support is not in place, how can you adapt?

Support, purpose, and determination will help you as you embark on changing your assessment practice. The ideas suggested above helped with the Feedback for Learning project, and ideally, in order for the changes to be sustainable, support is important. Others will want to participate when they realize the drastic changes in student success as they become independent student learners, thanks to assessment for learning.

4

SMALL Rs

The habits and skills of self-assessment are within the grasp and capabilities of almost every student.

— Chappuis and Stiggins, 2002

Guiding Questions

1. How would you treat the student who frequently has very little work completed as a student learner?

2. In assessment for learning classrooms, when is it correct to just tell a student what to do?

3. How will you get feedback for yourself on how long you wait for student responses?

Key Ideas of Chapter Four

- steps 4–7 transfer the responsibility for solving problems to the student

- steps 4–7 are a structure for the daily conversations between teacher and students

- an invitation must be respectful of the learner

- thinking takes time. Students need to be given time to respond

- teachers must restate the thinking process for the student

Introduction

Students need daily opportunities to experience reflective behaviour: hearing others making reflective statements, reading statements shared by other students, being guided by teachers, and observing the teacher coach other students. Each one of these experiences is a mini-reflection, a "small r," which adds to the students' metacognitive concepts and language. The accumulation of these experiences and skills prepares students to be successful with step 8, the "big R" (see figure 1.3), which asks students to reflect on themselves as learners.

As a very gifted teacher said to us, "The most important strategy for our students is practice, practice, practice." (Linda Pisa, Resource DL)

Students need to "practise, practise, practise" the skill of reflecting.

Let's take a moment to review our journey to create independent student learners. Steps 1–3 are designed to help students meet part a) of our definition: Recognize what they know or what they can do. (See chapter 2.) Steps 1–3 help teachers clarify learning targets for students so that more students experience daily success and thereby come to realize they do have knowledge and talents.

In this chapter, we will discuss how teachers can help students meet the second two parts of our definition of a student learner:

- identify what they are unsure of, or have difficulty with

- identify their next steps or have strategies to help them with their difficulties

Steps 4–7

Steps 4–7 of our scaffolding frame help teachers support students when they get stuck. In this sequence, students are taught how to look at their work critically, compare their work with the target model, and adjust their work so that they will be more successful.

Some students in grades 4–6 seem to have a talent for getting stuck. They also like to demonstrate this talent when the classroom is the busiest. Among this type of student are the squeaky wheels and the mournful moaners. Both these types have learned in their short school careers to deal with their problems by relying on the teacher. Other students in this group don't really have a problem – they just act as though they do in order to get attention and reassurance from their teacher.

On the other hand, there are students who avoid getting the teacher's attention. They are expert at avoiding the teacher's eye and getting lost in the commotion of the classroom. These students have weak skills and have learned to take very few risks. They think it is better to be silent and do nothing than to try something and be told it is wrong.

All teachers have strategies and routines to meet these student needs; unfortunately, the student requests for attention never occur one at a time: students' needs seem to erupt at the same time.

Faced with an onslaught of student demands, it is no wonder that teachers often resort to just "telling." With the teaching goal clearly in mind, the teacher might cruise through the room, telling students how to improve their work: "A capital is missing here." "You have missed something there." "Look at that line again." These statements direct students towards the target task. The resulting product is of high quality.

The students, however, are not required to rethink their work in terms of the target. The teacher has done the thinking for them, has spotted the error and used the force of the student/teacher relationship to sweep the student along to the conclusion. This is very efficient and many very good products will be created. The student feels successful to the degree the teacher is pleased.

If the teacher chooses to use steps 4–7, the ownership of the learning is transferred to the student and the classroom looks quite different.

Many students who run into trouble don't know how to go back to the target information to help them sort out their problem. Teachers must guide students in the process of learning how to use targets to help their thinking when they need to improve their work or when they need to think through a problem.

The teacher first establishes what the student has done well in terms of the task, intent, and criteria. Specific achievements are recognized in terms of the student's own work. The student is invited to compare her/his work to the criteria or model. Time is allowed for the thinking to occur. The student is helped by the teacher's focusing questions. More time is allowed. The student chooses the next step, however humble it may be. The student is commended for acting like a learner: choosing how to improve the assignment. The student feels successful because of the self-esteem that comes from ownership of one's actions.

The scaffolding (see figure 1.3) identifies four steps that help teachers turn over responsibility for problem solving to their students.

Step 4 Provide a first attempt for the students to show what they know.

Step 5 Invite comparison.

Step 6 Have students identify the next step(s).

Step 7 Provide an opportunity for a second attempt to reach the goals, using the chosen next step.

Steps 4–7 help students develop a pattern of thinking for reflecting on their daily work. Over time, students learn to see what gives them difficulty and how they prefer to deal with problems.

These four steps were the least understood by the teachers with whom we worked. They saw the four steps in terms of providing time for students to make improvements to their writing or to correct their mistakes. Step 5, "the invitation," meant telling the students, in a polite way, to begin editing or correcting. Teachers became very frustrated because they found that many students simply weren't interested in improving their work.

The teachers' frustration caused us to look more closely at the steps so that we were better able to understand the delicate handing off of responsibility for learning to the student.

We will discuss each step briefly and then show you how teachers have successfully implemented these steps.

Step 4: Provide a first attempt for the students to show what they know

In general, the first attempt occurs after the teacher stops talking. A lesson has been given, the task/intent/criteria written out, questions discussed, pencils sharpened. Students must have some opportunity to begin the task and complete as much as they can independently.

The teacher's role in step 4 is to step back, observe, and allow students the opportunity to work. This directive is simple but often difficult to achieve. There is a transition time between the lesson and the class's getting settled into their work. During this time, teachers will act to maintain order, help struggling students, and motivate those who are slow to get started.

The problem is that the transition time in many classrooms extends throughout the entire time students are working. Students in grades 4–6 have a rhythm to their work that invites teacher intervention. Grades 4–6 students are not always silent, diligent workers. They begin working, get off topic, come back to work, get silly with a friend, then come back to their work again. It is very easy for teachers to misinterpret students' actions unless a teacher allows time to observe the rhythms of student learning. The intent of this step is to allow students to work into problems – to get stuck – in the safety of the classroom. If all the students are successful, well and good, but the problems that may arise are learning opportunities as well.

We found that teachers could not just stand back and wait, so we suggest two ideas to help teachers make observations in their classrooms. The first suggestion is the *two-minute sweep*. Teachers tell the students, "No questions for two minutes, please." During the two minutes, teachers sweep their eyes around the class – without commenting (unless death or injury is imminent) – and just observe the students.

Teachers should be looking for success: Who is on task? Who is doing exactly what the assignment requires? Teachers should note exactly what the students are doing that is successful. When the two minutes are up, teachers go over to at least three students and compliment them. Not just general statements – "Good job" or "Way to go" – but specific and descriptive statements in terms of the criteria the class has set for a successful assignment: "I noticed you were using the spelling list to check your words," or "You shared the materials in our science class with your group. We said we should be helping each other and you did that by sharing." In addition to being a positive boost to the teacher's day, this activity keeps the teacher occupied and lets the students get on with their work.

Our second suggestion is to *survey*. Again, the intent is to give teachers a focus that distracts them from solving student problems too quickly. In this exercise, teachers record their observations about student learning. Teachers should guide their observations using a set of questions. These questions will differ, depending on the needs of the class, but teachers might begin the observation/ recording process with the following questions: What evidence is there about the preferred learning modalities of your students? What evidence is there of student understanding? What are student attitudes toward the task? These systematic observations can form the basis of teachers' decisions about adapting their approach to meet their students' needs.

Step 5: Invite comparison

There are only two words in this step, but each carries several implications. The word *invite* was carefully chosen to capture the respect for the learner that is necessary here. Students need to feel the teacher is not judgmental at this point, but supportive and understanding of their position. Teachers are helping students remember solutions or strategies that students might use.

The second word of step 5 also needs attention. "To compare" means we compare the students' work to some standard: the task/intent/criteria (TICs) for the lesson, student examples of the finished task, a teacher-created version, or models or lists of vocabulary, ideas, pictures.

Many students run into difficulties because they haven't remembered all the instructions. In these cases, teachers can help students by simply reminding them to read over the TICs of the lesson. Often, this is enough to help students think through their problem and find a solution.

We called a *wall expectation* any resource that teachers might post in their rooms to help students be independent. In assessment for learning classrooms, we expected to see the walls filled with learning tools.

One especially good resource for helping students be independent learners is the *strategy chart*. The intent of strategy charts is to expand the students' repertoire of how to help themselves beyond asking the teacher and using the TIC sheets. As strategies are introduced to students over the term, practised, and discussed some more, a list is compiled on large chart paper. If the students have worked with webs to organize their thinking, then "Webs" would go on the list. The list of ideas in figure 4.1 was compiled over time with the students and the teacher.

Figure 4.1 is a list used by a grade 5/6 class who was working in math on a unit on graphing. The teacher also posted a list of criteria for making a bar graph and the criteria for making a line plot graph to help students in their math project. The strategy list was there to help students when they didn't know what to do next. When students came to the teacher with a problem, she asked them if they had read over the classroom strategy chart to see if they could find an idea there. Usually this instruction was enough for the students to deal with the problem themselves. The list applied to more subjects than just math because the strategies could help students' thinking in many situations.

STRATEGIES
- THINKING BUBBLES
- ASK YOUR PARTNER
- ASK ANOTHER GROUP
- ASK A T.A.
- LOOK AT GRAPH POSTERS
- VENN DIAGRAM
- A WEB
- 4 QUADRANTS
- LOOK AT MATH BOOK
- LOOK AT CRITERIA CHARTS
- USE A T CHART
- USE A TABLE
- RE-READ DIRECTION SHEET
- BRAINSTORM
- USE QUICKWORD BOOK OR A DICTIONARY

Figure 4.1 Strategy chart. *Amie Johnson, grade 5/6.*

Step 6: Have students identify the next step

This step makes clear that assessment for learning requires the student to choose what must be changed or modified to improve their work. For students to be successful in identifying their next steps, they need time to make the choice and a range of options from which to choose. Students will not choose to do something that is beyond their capability and they will not make changes they consider trivial and uninteresting.

The changes students make will vary with their ability levels. Some students will need very small steps and others need challenging options. The next step for some students may be to spend more time trying to solve the problem by taking a new approach. An appropriate choice may be to choose a favourite strategy to help their thinking: talk to a friend, use a web, or refer to a wall chart. When students are identifying their next steps, the teacher must be patient, positive, and able to use appropriate questions to help the student's thinking.

Step 7: Provide an opportunity for a second attempt to reach the goal(s), using the chosen next step

Steps 6 and 7 should happen with minimal time in between. When students see something they can do to improve their work, they like to make the changes immediately. The student learns that their decisions and actions bring improvement to their work. Success is not a chance occurrence beyond the student's control but a result of her/his actions. Teachers need to ensure that students have class time to make the changes.

The down side of such quick action is that the action may not be remembered by the student. Teachers also must help students to remember what changes they decided to make.

The pattern of steps 4–7 begins with students working with minimal interruption by the teacher. If students encounter difficulties, then the teacher helps the students consider options available to them and allows the students time to think carefully and make their own decisions. Once the students have decided what to do, they are allowed to make immediate changes to their work.

Many teachers implement steps 4–7 using *written reflections* to "invite" students to think about their work.

In one school, three of the classes worked together on a statistics unit. The grades 4, 5, and 6 classes were collecting data on the eating habits of the students in their school. The students devised questions and then interviewed the school population to gather their data. The teachers were careful to help students with strategies they could use to make the interviews successful: give suggestions, talk louder, reread more slowly, walk away and come back later.

Students were given a chance to "pause and think" after their interviews (see figure 4.2).

This example of a "pause and think" reflection shows how writing can help students make the strategies active parts of their learning. The reflection is in terms of the established learning targets: strategies used to help themselves. The student notes something she has to pay attention to, "talking clearly," and a strategy used, "talking louder." Asking students to put their reflections in writing helps them put a shape to their learning experiences that might otherwise be lost. The written reflections can also be saved and reviewed by students at a later day.

> Today is the first time I did my survey.
> I surveyed Jessica. I thought it was fun because
> I got to know what she eat's for breakfast and
> if she eat's breakfast. Something I noticed about
> asking a questions is that I have to talk clearly.
> The strategy I followed was talking flouder.

Figure 4.2 Pause and think strategy. *Teresa Campanelli, Reynu Gill, Marnie Olsen, grades 4/5/6.*

> The "pause and think" strategy comes from the books by Kathleen Gregory, Caren Cameron, and Anne Davies (1997, 2000, 2001). Teachers found these books extremely helpful. These books contain many concrete techniques that promote assessment for learning.

Many teachers had students compare their work to rubrics. Rubrics are often used by teachers to help guide their marking and evaluation, and can also be used by students as a tool to help them improve their work.

A rubric was posted on chart paper at the introduction of a lesson. This was followed by each student doing an activity based on the lesson to prove that he/she understood the curriculum content. After, each student filled in a self-reflection sheet based on the rubric. Students decided from their reflection areas they needed to get better at. Throughout the year students kept reflecting on specific aspects of their learning (e.g. graphs). They found that they were getting better and better!

– Luciano Mota, grade 3/4

Children filled out a rubric as they completed three writing jobs to assess their stories. They used a highlighter to mark directly on the rubric to give them a clear visual of what they had accomplished and how they had improved. Then they used the three rubrics to make goals for their next writing project.

– Kathleen Weir, grade 4

In both cases the teachers repeatedly drew the students' attention back to the learning target so that the students could learn how to assess their own work and make adjustments for improvements.

Teachers can also use rubrics to help students develop a sense of ownership for their work and a sense of pride in doing their best work.

In a grade 5/6 class, the students were working on a research project on explorers. After some discussion, the students helped the teacher devise the rubric to be used to guide their work. As the students worked in groups, the teachers would continually draw the students' attention to the rubric they had first created.

> Let's look at the rubric and see if we're on track. Is there anything we have to change in our product or in our rubric?
>
> — *James Gray, grade 5/6*

Most of the time, students responded, "I'm on track." The reminder helped the students monitor their progress.

One of the groups found a map of an explorer's journey and showed it to the class. As a result of the discussion, the class agreed the original rubric for the project should now include "maps" as a category.

The impact on this particular class was impressive. Up to this point, the teacher felt "I was at my wit's end" because the students were having trouble struggling with working in their groups. The teacher realized that the students' discomfort was part of their learning how to work in groups, but worried that this difficulty would interfere with their research. When the students saw the teacher adapt the rubric according to their suggestion, "There was a shift in understanding in what they had to do."

At the teacher's lowest point, a group of students came to him to ask, "Can we work on our explorer project today?" and another asked, "Can I take it home to work on?" The groups began to be more cohesive when students began to take more ownership of the research. The teacher's perseverance and willingness to adapt the learning goals resulted in students' increasing their self-esteem as learners (see figure 4.3). Their reflective comments show how strongly they felt about their work.

Creating Independent Student Learners

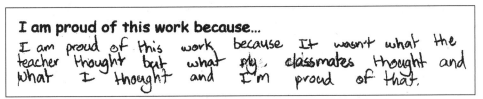

> **I am proud of this work because...**
>
> I am proud of this work because It wasn't what the teacher thought but what my classmates thought and what I thought and I'm proud of that.

Figure 4.3 Reflective comments. *Student from James Gray's grade 5/6 class.*

At some point a rubric becomes fixed, but teachers must be open to refining the original to reflect how the students' inquiry had led them to new understandings.

One art teacher used a series of questions to help her students improve their work. Lidi Kuiper is a master teacher who developed a questioning technique before she began working on assessment for learning. She recognized immediately the connection between her own thinking about using questions to help students improve their work in art and the ideas of assessment for learning.

After a brief lesson, the students are encouraged to begin working on the art lesson for the day. When the students are about halfway through their work or when they have declared, "I'm finished," the teacher displays all the students' work. The teacher helps the students look carefully at each work by using descriptive language to describe each work. Then the art teacher uses questions to direct the students' attention to particular aspects of the displayed artwork.

> Which artwork shows that the artist took care with …?

The students review all the work displayed and find the variety of ways other students have solved the problem of the assignment. The students see the range of options available to them for their own work. At this point, the teacher gives the students a chance to make changes to their own work.

> Now, look back at your own work. If you are happy with how you used the tools and materials, give yourself a "thumbs-up." If you can think of something you would like to add to your work to make it better, nod to yourself.

Ms Kuiper reports, "[The students] invariably return to their work after the talk to do more and to improve their art pieces."

This example from an art class demonstrates very clearly that when students have a range of choices and time to decide what best suits them, they naturally turn to their own work to make improvements.

All our examples of teacher work follow the pattern of steps 4–7. The teachers allowed students to work on their own with minimal support. The written reflections, rubrics, and questions invited students to think about their work in terms of some external standard. Students were given time to think about their experiences and compare them to the standard. Teachers stepped back so that the students made their own choices about how to improve their work.

Learning Conversations

The tendency for teachers is to see written assignments as the primary way for students to reflect on the quality of their efforts and a way not to think about the daily momentary exchanges between themselves and their students. Often, very little attention is paid to the nature of teachers' talk with students. Even though teachers spend most of their class time engaged in conversations with groups or individual students, teachers spend little time thinking about how to use these conversations as opportunities for students to have mini-reflections about their learning. Teachers should think about steps 4–7 in terms of how they talk to students every day.

Step 4 Students are allowed to get started on their work and, as they have problems, they come up to the teacher.

Step 5 Students are made to feel at ease – they feel "invited" and then they are asked to "compare."

Step 6 Teachers step back and wait while students choose their next steps.

Step 7 Teachers ask students to restate the problem before they go on to continue their work.

When we observed teachers, it was obvious they cared about their students and were interested in what they had to say. Teachers showed their concern in their body language, the words they used, and the tone of the conversations. When we talked to these teachers about "how" they talked to students, they felt it was obvious: "you just talk to them." We could see that the teachers' manner of asking students to compare their work to a set target and the quality of the teachers' questions are important.

> The "Learning Conversation" is an adaptation of the work of Costa and Garmston, 2002.

To help teachers intuit about how to make conversations with students more explicit, we rewrote steps 4–7 to more clearly apply to their daily conversations. We began to call the daily use of these steps in teacher-student conversations *learning conversations*.

We will begin our discussion of learning conversations with a transcription of a recorded conversation in the grade 4/5/6 classroom of Teresa Campanelli. The students needed to work in pairs to display the work they had been doing on chart paper. The intent was to make a rough draft so that the information could be presented to the class and discussed. The criteria were written on the board: clear, complete, well organized.

As the students worked, they would come up to the teacher with problems they faced. The following is the slightly edited conversation between Ms Campanelli and Sonja, a grade 4 student. The conversation took about two and half minutes.

Teacher: Sonja, tell me what problem you're having organizing your data.
Sonja: I came to ask if this is all right with you.

Teacher: How do you mean, 'all right'?
Sonja: (Indicating with her hand) Do you want us to change anything?

Teacher: Is this like a checkpoint for you?
Sonja: (Nods)

Teacher: When I look at this, it looks pretty clear. How will you know when you're done?
Sonja: When I have all the questions on there.

Teacher: So not all the questions are on there.
Sonja: I just came to ask you if this is all right.

Teacher: You came to ask if you're on the right track. How do you know if you're on track? How can you tell?

Sonja: I don't know.

Teacher: Let's look at the criteria. (Pointing to the word on the list) It had to be clear.

Sonja: I didn't know if this was clear enough or not.

Teacher: Oh. (Pausing to think about the student's answer)

Sonja: It was clear enough for me. I didn't know if it was clear enough for you.

Teacher: It's clear enough in that it looks legible. I like the use of colour. It looks appealing to me. So, I answered your question?

Sonja: (Nods)

Teacher: What are doing with this? (Indicating the chart paper)

Sonja: We're gonna put it up for the class.

Teacher: All the other students will be looking at it. Here's another way to tell if it's clear. You could do it by yourself. I could hold it for you and you stand back there and tell me if it's clear enough. Okay. (Teacher holds the paper and the student moves a few metres away.) You go take a look. Can you read it?

Sonja: (Nods)

Teacher: I think you've solved your problem. I told you why I thought it was clear and gave you another to strategy you could use on your own. (Looking at Sonja's eyes). Do you feel good about going back and continuing?

Sonja: (Smiles, nods more vigorously, and returns to her desk to work)

Sonja is just in the early stages of her journey to being an independent student. The conversation begins with a very common question: Is this all right? Her teacher refines her thinking about her problem and models the language of an independent learner.

The student is welcomed: Is this like a checkpoint for you?
The student is asked to be specific: How do you mean, 'all right'?

The student's general words are made specific: "Is it all right with the teacher?" becomes "Is it clear?"
The teacher used specific words of quality – "legible" and "use of colour" – to build the student's learning vocabulary.

Questions shift the child's thinking about the problem: "How do you know when you are done?"
The student's attention is turned directly to the criteria sheet.
The student's words are paraphrased before a response is made: "So not all the questions are on there."
The teacher extends the student's repertoire of strategies: "Here's another way to tell."

The teacher summarizes the conversation: I told you why I thought it was clear and I gave you another strategy.
The teacher pays close attention to the student's personal satisfaction: (looking at the student's eyes) Do you feel good about going back?

The teacher also understood intuitively when to stop asking questions. When the student didn't know what "clear" meant to the teacher, the teacher responded with specific criteria. The teacher did not ask the student what she thought "clear" meant. This had not been discussed in the original instructions and it was a reasonable question by the student.

As these conversations are repeated throughout the day and during the school year, the students do more of the talking and the teacher's participation is reduced to using a few strategic questions. The Learning Conversation Frame (see figure 4.4) lists the important elements of a teacher/student learning conversation.

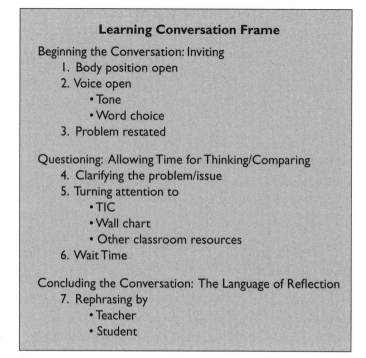

Learning Conversation Frame

Beginning the Conversation: Inviting
  1. Body position open
  2. Voice open
    • Tone
    • Word choice
  3. Problem restated

Questioning: Allowing Time for Thinking/Comparing
  4. Clarifying the problem/issue
  5. Turning attention to
    • TIC
    • Wall chart
    • Other classroom resources
  6. Wait Time

Concluding the Conversation: The Language of Reflection
  7. Rephrasing by
    • Teacher
    • Student

Figure 4.4 Learning conversation frame.

Beginning the conversation: the invitation to think

The intent of the first part of the learning conversation is to establish the teacher's respect for the student as a learner. The teacher's tone and the body language are as important as the words. The basic message to the student should be, "It is okay to have a problem."

The overall message we want to give to students is that we are all learners, we all get stuck, and, if we are learning something new, of course we will run into problems. When a student comes to the teacher with a question, the first need is to help the student clarify the problem. Some questions might be:

- Can you tell me what's wrong?
- What's the problem?
- Where are you stuck?

Paraphrasing shows you are listening and care what the student has to say. It is one more way of establishing a respectful tone to the conversation.

Questions for comparison: allowing thinking time

The intent in this section is to ask the student to 'think back' to possible resources in the classroom that might help solve the problem.

The invitation to think about the problem begins with asking the student what they have tried already, implying that the student has previously tried several approaches and has run out of ideas. The teacher must listen and decide if the student has understood the task at hand. Perhaps the student needs only to be helped to go over the instructions. If the student is clear on the instructions but is still stuck, the teacher can "invite comparison" to the wall chart of thinking strategies that the student might use to help solve the problem.

A big challenge for teachers at this stage is to wait for the response after a question is asked. This takes a great deal of practice on the part of the teacher.

For many very good reasons, wait time after questions is abandoned by teachers. We believe one of the reasons teachers don't wait for students to respond is that teachers want students to succeed. If the student doesn't answer the question in less than a second, the teacher asks another question and then another to find the right words to help make the student successful. Unfortunately, this only results in confusing the student, who is still back at the first question. At this point the teacher usually tells the student what to do. The "telling" is phrased like a suggestion: "Do you think you could ...?" The student understands this is a command, coded in teacher talk, not an invitation.

After the teacher asks the question, the teacher must stop talking. We have often thought that it would be very helpful if, in the English language, questions were followed by the tag, "And now I'm going to stop talking for five seconds to give you a chance to respond."

So the question should really be:

> Can you tell me what's wrong? I'm going to stop talking for five seconds to give you a chance to respond.

This tag would be a constant reminder to the teacher that a question is meant to be an invitation to think and that a response will take time to formulate. Invariably, when we talk to teachers about waiting for the student to answer, they shake their heads and smile in recognition of the need for waiting and the recognition that they don't wait long enough. It is a problem for you to train yourself to wait but very important to students to have time to organize their thinking, to find the right words, and then to tell you the answer. The teacher can help the student by rephrasing the student's statements and gently probing with further questions until both teacher and student feel they have zeroed in on the problem.

The teacher's next step is to turn the student's attention to classroom resources that might help. One of the first resources to explore is the original instruction given to the student.

The question should be framed positively so that it builds on the student's strengths:

> When we started, we talked about what to do. Can you tell me what you remember?

In a similar fashion, teachers can invite students to think about other resources in the room they might use: strategy lists, vocabulary lists, or student samples. Teachers can also encourage students to think back to previous experiences that have useful similarities. Students then can choose what to do next as they review the most helpful resource.

With questions, the teacher helps the student compare her/his present thinking to the list of strategies compiled over the school year. If teachers think of the questions of terms of drawing the students' attention to the resources or reminders of what is available, then the questions will be framed positively. The student will hear the questions as invitations.

> Do you think you can find a strategy that might help your thinking?
> Have you another strategy you like from the list you might use now?

Often, students need help learning how to look at the resource. The teacher may have to direct the student's attention to particular aspects of the instructions to help the student concentrate on one part. Repeatedly referring students to the strategy list trains students in how to use the list as a problem-solving resource.

Each time the teacher patiently leads the student through this process, the student is practising reflective thinking. The message to the student is that when you are learning, not everything will be easy but you can be successful, and that you have to think about how to help yourself. Students learn that when they are confronted with a problem, they can use a variety of strategies to come to a solution.

Concluding the conversation: building the language of reflection

The intent here is to help students develop the language of reflection. Once the student sees what to do, the problem disappears. The student's mind jumps from stuck to unstuck without any intervening time spent thinking about what just happened; the student just wants to fix the problem. The teacher can help the students reflect by asking, "So how did you solve (or are going to solve) the problem?"

> The ideas for concluding the conversation came from Teresa Campanelli, grade 5/6, who, when practising the Learning Conversation with a student, said, "Just so I know that you and I agree, can you tell me what the solution is?"

The first few times, the teacher may have to supply the answer but, as the process is repeated, more and more students will be able to answer the question fully and the teacher's role will be reduced to listening and asking questions.

Art talk

We have already discussed above the work of one art teacher, Lidi Kuiper. Ms Kuiper created a pattern of questioning to help her students, which she called "Art Talk." This series of questions was a combination of Bloom's taxonomy, the Feldman discussion model, and her own experience. The quality of questions is important when teachers are "inviting comparison" between what they have done and a model or some other example. The questions from Art Talk lead the student to higher level thinking about their work.

Although the questions (see figure 4.5) are designed for students working in art, the pattern in the question series can be transferred to other subjects as well. The students are helped to describe their own work. Students are questioned while they work to think about options. Students are encouraged to stretch their thinking about how they are considering their work, and they are asked to identify their strengths. Finally, students are helped to consolidate their learning by thinking back on their experience.

Art Talk: Teacher and Student Talking about Art Work

Getting Started	How do you feel about getting started on your art work? Tell me about your ideas for what you want to make. What part of the … would you like to make first? I see you already have … in your picture. What would you like to do next?
While Working	What materials/techniques have you used? How do you like using these materials/this technique? Would you like help with …? Tell me what you know about … What do you want to show in your work? What could you try? What has worked before when you had trouble?
Almost Finished	How do you feel about this part of your picture? What would you change if you had to change just one thing? What if you had to start all over? Would you do anything differently? Why did you choose this colour/texture/shape, etc.? How did you create this effect? Which is the most detailed part of your work? Can you think of another part that could use more detail? Let's look at your work from across the room. Is the emphasis where you want it to be? Is there enough contrast? Let's look at your work upside down. Is the composition still balanced? What is your work about? Do you want your work to tell a story or have a message? What part of the project did you enjoy most?
Finished	What techniques worked best for you? What did you try that you've never tried before? What is the most/least successful part of your project? What would you do differently if you could do the project again? Where did you get your ideas? Is this connected to other things you are learning? What did you learn the most about? Can you use what you have learned for something else?

Figure 4.5 Art talk. *Lidi Kuiper, grades 4, 5, 6.*

Collegiality: An Essay

Teaching is a lonely job. When you close the door to your classroom, the success of the students lies directly on your shoulders. Most of the time, having the responsibility for the group of learners is a rewarding challenge. In the classroom, there are multiple opportunities to experience the world of the child through conversations with your students. But, there is also a need for adult conversation.

Adult learners need to be able to talk with colleagues in order to develop in their profession. Thoughts that are a jumble of emotions, reactions, and intent become clearer as you try to express them in the linear fashion of a conversation. Conversations that enhance your learning should be thoughtful and reflective about your job. You must feel you are being listened to, respected, and supported.

There are times in your teaching career when you are blessed with the wonderful happenstance of working alongside a soulmate, a person who shares many of your values and dreams for teaching. Such a friend adds a quality to your workplace that cannot be measured. You can express your frustration, confusion, and excitement, and know that your feelings will be met with sympathy, encouragement, and good humour. These conversations can be very brief and happen during the school day or can be extended planning sessions over weekend getaways.

Not all your professional relationships will be this special, nor do they need to be. It is still possible to have rich and meaningful dialogue with colleagues who have different responsibilities or experiences but are sympathetic and want to learn about their profession.

You will not grow as a teacher if you do not have many opportunities to talk over your ideas with a variety of colleagues. Reading educational materials and working by yourself can only take you so far. It is difficult to step outside yourself, pause, and ask, "What have I learned?" A group of colleagues can help you analyze the problems you face, sharpen your understanding, and, just as importantly, they can help you celebrate your successes.

Formal opportunities that allow teachers to engage in reflective conversations are rare. There are many times when a teacher can grab moments from their daily obligations to exchange a few words with a co-worker, but there are very few times when teachers are permitted to sit with colleagues and reflect on the effectiveness of their programs or the nuances of their mandate.

Momentary exchanges while you are between tasks or the students are out at recess do not count as opportunities to learn. You cannot have really meaningful dialogue while you are in the classroom, even if the students are engaged in some project work. There are too many distractions for the conscientious teacher. Staff meetings are not an ideal time, either. These meetings usually occur at the end of the day, when you have already expended much of your energy teaching, and often have packed agendas that must be covered in short periods of time.

The talk must occur when you are rested, and without distractions, and be long enough that you can delve into the topic. We suggest putting aside at least 30 minutes. With these conditions, you have a chance to begin thinking about your practice.

From time to time, teachers are given opportunities to share ideas at in-service days and, infrequently, meetings are scheduled during the regular school days. The learning can be removed from these opportunities for discussion if the meetings have been over-organized or are about administrative issues. Often these meetings are chaired by an administrator and are structured around the need to organize specific school events. Interesting conversations such as on-topic personal asides or exploration of interesting sidebars are kept to a minimum. Meetings organized in this way have administrative value but do not really help teachers learn their craft.

Collegial conversations for teacher learning require a different structure. The general responsibility for the discussion should lie with the group. The chairperson has the permission of the participants to bring everyone back on topic but is not too authoritative. The tone of the meeting allows the participants to talk about the issues that they face, their stumbling blocks, and their frustrations.

In these very democratic conversations, ideas flow back and forth in a spirit of camaraderie. They are driven by a sense of inquiry into an area in which all the participants are interested. Teachers want to know what is going on in other classrooms. They want to know, "How is it organized?" "What topics are being covered at the moment?" "What are you trying that is successful?" As these ideas emerge, each teacher's understanding of the topic deepens. These conversations can be very exciting and rewarding for each individual. Conversations like these leave teachers with a sense that they know more about their craft.

Another teacher-support conversation is one where one teacher takes on the role of a mentor, coach, or a lead teacher. Most teachers shy away from this role because it sounds as if they are calling themselves a *master teacher* who will dispense wisdom to other teachers.

A coaching conversation between two colleagues deepens understanding by helping the teacher look back on their work and reflect. Teachers can take turns being the coach/listener and the teacher/speaker. These conversations should also take place outside the classroom, free of distractions, rather than in a busy staffroom at lunch hour.

The listener is not there to give advice but to help make the options clearer. Not having to give advice relieves the listener from the responsibility of providing the right answer. The listener is allowed to paraphrase what is said and to use questions to help the teacher be more specific and see what options are available.

The teacher who is speaking chooses the topic and agrees to avoid asking for solutions. Most teachers struggle to avoid asking for advice. Teachers who are really tired or under the pressure of a deadline will resort to, "Just tell me what to do!"

This model is also a safe way for teachers to visit each other's classroom. In this case the coach/listener watches and possibly gathers data on some issue identified by the teacher/speaker. After the observation, the only responsibility of the coach/listener is to report what was seen or to hand over the data collected. There is no need for the coach/listener to give judgments because their only responsibility is to provide another set of eyes. The purpose of the coach/listener model is to clarify the teacher's thinking. Ultimately, this is the best model since it leads the teachers to discover answers for themselves.

All these conversations have their strengths and weaknesses. All are needed if teachers are to develop in their profession as learners.

(These ideas are based on Costa and Garmston, 2002.)

APPENDICES

REPRODUCIBLES

Appendix 1:
Measuring Impact Form

Teacher:_____

School:_____ Grade:_____

1. What did you do? _____

   _____

   _____

   _____

2. To what extent did it work? _____

   _____

   _____

   _____

3. How do you know? (You may wish to include a description of the types
   of students who were most affected.)_____

   _____

   _____

   _____

4. Attachments: (work samples, marks, tape recording, videotapes, student-
   written comments, TA comments) _____

   _____

   _____

   _____

   _____

Creating Independent Student Learners

Appendix 2:
Short Planning Sheet for Scaffolding Assessment

Questions	Comments
Step 1: • The learning task and learning intent (why)	
Step 2: • How will task/intent be shared? • How will student ideas be recorded? • My own key criteria:	
Step 3: • Some enabling tasks to help students learn:	
Step 4: • How much time is allowed for students' first attempt?	
Step 5: • How will students be encouraged to compare their work to the standard? (worksheet, classmates, teacher) • What will I pay attention to when inviting comparison? (wait time, question type)	
Step 6: • What choices are there for students when they choose their next steps?	
Step 7: • How quickly can next steps be taken?	
Step 8: • How and when will students reflect as learners? • What questions will be asked?	

Appendix 3:
Planning Questions for Teachers

Part One: Getting Yourself Ready

1. What is the task? (Step 1: Task) _____

   _____

2. Why are you asking students to do this task? (Step 1: Intent)

   _____

   _____

3. How will you introduce the task and the intent? (a skit, grade-level presentation, school assembly, guest speaker) (Step 2: Sharing)

   _____

   _____

4. What criteria will indicate success? (Step 2: Sharing)

Looks Like / Sounds Like

What will it look like?	What will it sound like?

5. How will you involve the students in identifying the criteria? _____

6. What images or symbols can be associated with the items on the criteria list?

   _____

   _____

   _____

   _____

7. Where will the criteria sheet be posted in the room? _____

8. What skills will the students need in order to be successful? (Step 3: Enabling)

   _____

   _____

   _____

9. What enabling activities can the students use to learn and practise these skills? (Step 3: Enabling)

Skills	Enabling Activity

Part Two: Helping Students Learn

10. How will you invite students to compare their work with the list called Looks Like/Sounds Like? (Step 5: Invite, and Step 6: Student identifies)

a) Some time after students have started:

- What will you choose to say that is specific, descriptive, and related to the list called Looks Like/Sounds Like? _____

_____

_____

- How will you refer to the list when you ask the student to tell you her/his assessment of his/her work? _____

_____

_____

- How often will you ask students to write their comments down? (consider the learning style of the students, general writing ability)

_____

_____

- How will you help students build the vocabulary they need to record their evaluations? (word lists, model sentences, checklists with icons)

_____

_____

_____

b) After all students have had a chance to continue their work:

- Have a whole-class review of the list called Looks Like/Sounds Like.

- Which items on the list were the easiest to accomplish? _____

_____

Creating Independent Student Learners

- Which items on the list were the most difficult to accomplish?

  _____

  _____

- How might we help ourselves to do better?_____

  _____

  _____

- Are there items to add to or delete from our list? (teachers may also wish to add/delete items) _____

  _____

c) After students have completed their work:

- Ask students to present to one another and take turns pretending to be the teacher, listening to the student reading his/her work. Move through the classroom and note examples of students exhibiting behaviours that are on the target list. Afterwards, the students and teacher report examples of students hitting their target.

- Ask students to present to the class. Ask questions of the students, based on the list Looks Like/Sounds Like.

11. How quickly can you give students an opportunity to practise changing their work? (Step 7: Second attempt)_____

Some suggestions:

- Review with the students as you start the next assignment. Look at the successes, difficulties, and strategies from the previous assignments.

- Present a general issue to the class that you have observed. Ask the class to work in pairs to suggest solutions and share their ideas with the whole class.

- Ask permission to present one student's "difficulty" to the class and have the whole class suggest possible solutions. Then present the class with a similar, but different, "difficulty" and let the students practise one of the solutions in groups.

Part Three: Reviewing the Learning

12. How will you celebrate student progress and deepen their learning?

    (Step 8: Student learning) _____

    _____

    This should occur after the students have worked at several assignments, re-examined their performance, and tried to practise the skills they need to improve. For this to work most efficiently, students should review the accumulated evaluation sheets referred to in Part Two: Helping Students Learn.

    • What do you think you do especially well? _____

    _____

    • Describe the challenges. _____

    _____

    • What strategies did you choose to help you with the difficult parts? _____

    _____

    • How well did the strategies work? _____

    • What other strategies might you use? _____

    _____

    • Next time ... _____

    _____

    _____

Appendix 4:
Rubric for Success: How Am I Doing?

Step 1: Setting Goal(s)	Task and intent not clear	Teacher understands task and intent but these are framed in general terms	Intent and task stated in terms specific enough to guide teaching and assessing*
Step 2: Sharing with Students	Goals not stated	Teacher shares goals with students	Goals have been explained, illustrated, and exemplified in ways appropriate for students' learning profiles**
Step 3: Enabling Tasks	Learning activities do not connect with the learning intent	Some activities directed towards student success in meeting the intended skills and concepts	Most activities enable and encourage students to achieve and demonstrate intended skills and concepts
Step 3: Assessment Criteria	Assessment criteria not shared with students	Teacher provides the assessment criteria	Students are invited to develop criteria through discussion and use of exemplars
Step 4: First Attempt	Students unclear of purpose and criteria	Students clear about purpose, but criteria have not been reviewed	Students clear on purpose of task. Intent and criteria have been reviewed
Step 5: Inviting Comparison	Teacher's comment on the work is non-specific, evaluative (e.g., this is good, satisfactory, poor) rather than descriptive	Teacher comments on the work, referring to the assessment criteria	Teacher encourages students to reflect and comment on the work, referring to the assessment criteria
Step 6: Identifying Next Steps	Teacher provides general instructions for next steps	Teacher is directive, identifies next steps, and instructs students	Teacher encourages students to identify next step(s)
Step 7: Second Attempt	No second attempt offered	Students try again but are unclear about improvements needed	Students try again, clearly focused on what needs improvement and how to achieve it
Step 8: Students Looking Back	No attempt made to look back and recognize progress	Progress recognized but only in general terms	Teacher prompts students to recognize their learning and specific progress as a frequent routine, and over longer cycles of time

The intent can be explored after the task has been explained or even started: decisions about timing depend on the nature of the task, the learning preferences and profile of the students, and other circumstances.

Learning profile *is defined as including the student's cognitive, affective, psychomotor domains, developmental level, and learning style.*

BIBLIOGRAPHY

Assessment Reform Group. *Assessment for Learning Beyond the Black Box.* Cambridge, UK: University of Cambridge School of Education, [1999].

Bachman, R. *Any Road.* CD. Produced by Randy Bachman and Chris Wardman. © 1992 Ranbach Music. Distributed by Sony Music Canada, Inc.

Black, P., and D. Wiliam. "Inside the Black Box: Raising Standards Through Classroom Assessment." *Phi Delta Kappan* 80, No. 2 (October 1998): 139–148.

Chappuis, S., and R.J. Stiggins. "Classroom Assessment for Learning." *Educational Leadership.* Association for Supervision and Curriculum Development (September 2002): 40–43.

Clarke, S. *Targeting Assessment in the Primary Classroom: Strategies for Planning, Assessment, Pupil Feedback and Target Setting.* London, UK: Hodder and Stoughton, 1998.

_____. *Unlocking Formative Assessment: Practical Strategies for Enhancing Pupils' Learning in the Primary Classroom.* London, UK: Hodder and Stoughton, 2001.

Costa, A., and R. Garmston. *Cognitive Coaching: a Foundation for Renaissance Schools.* 2nd ed. Norwood, MA: Christopher-Gordon, 2002.

Costa, A.L., and B. Kallick. "Learning Through Reflection." In *Habits of Mind: A Developmental Series.* Book III, *Assessing and Reporting on Habits of Mind.* Alexandria, VA: Association for Supervision and Curriculum, 2000.

Davies, A. *Making Classroom Assessment Work*. Courtenay, BC: Connections Publishing, 2000.

Davies, A., C. Cameron, C. Politano, and K. Gregory. *Together Is Better: Collaborative Assessment, Evaluation, and Reporting*. Winnipeg, MB: Peguis Publishing, 1992.

Fogarty, R., and J. Stoehr. *Integrating Curricula with Multiple Intelligences Teams, Themes and Threads*. Palatine, IL: Skylight, 1995.

Gregory, K., C. Cameron, and A. Davies. *Knowing What Counts*. Vol. 1, *Setting and Using Criteria*. Courtenay, BC: Connections Publishing, 1997.

_____. *Knowing What Counts*. Vol. 2, *Self Assessment and Goal Setting*. Courtenay, BC: Connections Publishing, 2000.

_____. *Knowing What Counts*. Vol. 3, *Conferencing and Reporting*. Courtenay, BC: Connections Publishing, 2001.

Sutton, R. *Assessment for Learning*. Salford, UK: RS Publications, 1995.

_____. *The Learning School*. Salford, UK: RS Publications, 1998.

Stiggins, R. *Student-Centered Classroom Assessment*. 2nd ed. Columbus, Ohio: Merrill Publishing, 1997.

Wiggins, G. *Educative Assessment: Designing Assessments to Inform and Improve Student Performance*. San Francisco, CA: Jossey-Bass Publishers, 1998.

Wiggins, G., and J. McTighe. *Understanding by Design*. 2nd ed. Alexandria, VA: Association for Supervision and Curriculum Development, 2005.